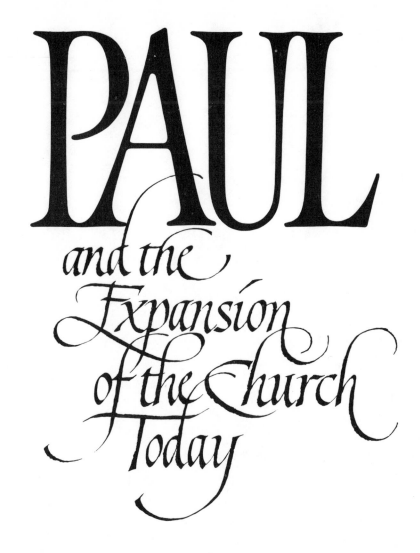

PAUL
and the Expansion of the Church Today

EDWIN BROWN FIRMAGE

Deseret Book Company
Salt Lake City, Utah
1979

Library of Congress Cataloging in Publication Data

Firmage, Edwin Brown.
    Paul and the expansion of the Church today.

    Bibliography, p.
    Includes index.
    1. Paul, Saint, apostle.   2. Missions—Biblical
teaching.   3. Church of Jesus Christ of Latter-day
Saints—Missions.   I. Title.
BS2506.F54   266'.0092'4   79-21235
ISBN 0-87747-789-2

Contents

Preface

This slim volume is dedicated to my grandfather, Elder Hugh B. Brown, a man I dearly love and admire. His was a Pauline spirit— and still is. He shared the vision of a gospel message universal in time and space. It is a gospel as necessary for the restless, alienated, and lonely victim of the industrial world of the twentieth century as it was for the Jewish Christian of the first century, who faced the destruction of his nation's Holy City, or the Saint in Rome, enduring Nero's persecution; it is as helpful today to a citizen of a central African state as to a person whose heritage is western European.

The basis of Grandfather's universal spirit, like Paul's, was his understanding and application of Christian love. To him the Fatherhood of God was a reality, not simply a trite saying. And the implications of this doctrine made it necessary for Grandfather to embrace the principles of universal love and brotherhood. He saw too many of his neighbor's characteristics, both good and bad, in his own soul to allow him to do other than regard his neighbor as himself. He considered it a logical impossibility to do otherwise.

That Pauline characteristic of Christian love was described in the following tribute I offered at Grandfather's death:

Preeminent perhaps in a man endowed with so many natural gifts was his capacity to love. His was an unconditional love, like that of the Master whom he served. He did not demand as a prerequisite to his love that the recipient be a perfect person, for Grandfather understood that that would eliminate anyone to love.

His love extended beyond the boundaries we too often enclose ourselves within as we choose whom we should love. His love extended beyond church membership; across racial or national divisions. He loved us sinners, and saints wherever they could be found. He understood the problem of motes and beams. He left judgment to the Lord.

Grandfather lived to see a great expansion of the Church. His lifespan stretched from the presidency of John Taylor to that of Spencer W. Kimball. But Grandfather did not live to see the many developments and extensions of the Church that have dramatically taken place under President Kimball's leadership. In a sense, Grandfather served as did Stephen and Philip, as one who helped prepare the way for greater things to come. President Kimball has become the Pauline spirit of our time. His humility has allowed the Holy Spirit to whisper words of universal love, a solvent that works to dissolve away the barriers of race, ideology, or nationality with which we divide ourselves from each other. Accordingly, I feel it is appropriate that we quote Spencer W. Kimball as the introduction to this book. His words express his vision of the importance of carrying the Master's gospel "unto the uttermost part of the earth." (Acts 1:8.)

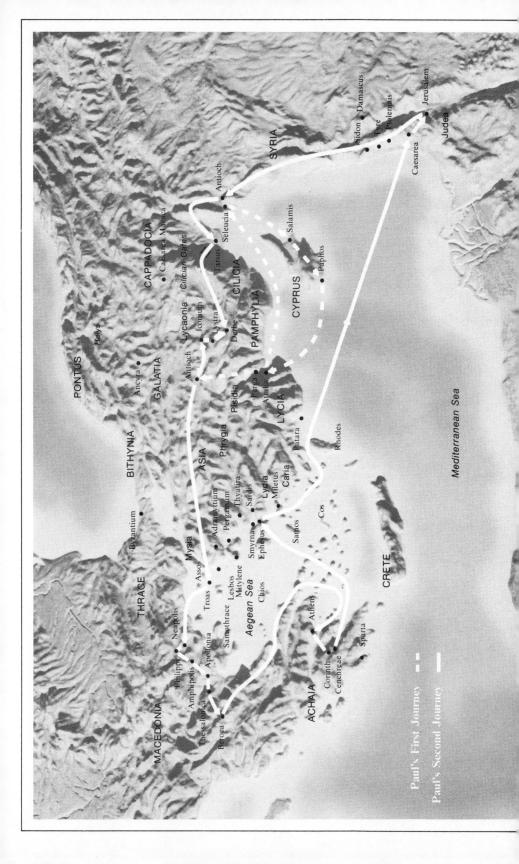

Paul's First Journey - - -
Paul's Second Journey ———

Paul's Third Journey

A Call to Prepare

"It seems as though the Lord is moving upon the affairs of men and of nations to hasten the day of the readiness when leaders will permit the elect among them to receive the gospel of Jesus Christ and when the gospel will be preached 'for a witness' among all nations. . . .

"We can bring the gospel with its healing balm and its powerful programs to countless numbers, not only to introduce the gospel to them but to show them in our communities how we live and how they can live and better their lives. . . . The Lord by his Spirit is preparing people for the day when the gospel will be taught them in plainness. We must be ready.

"There are almost three billion people now living on the earth in nations where the gospel is not now being preached. If we could only make a small beginning in every nation, soon the converts among each kindred and tongue could step forth as lights to their own people and the gospel would thus be preached in all nations before the coming of the Lord." (President Spencer W. Kimball, from an address delivered at the Regional Representatives seminar, September 29, 1978. See *Ensign*, July 1979, pp. 2-9.)

Chapter One

Paul the Man

This book is about Paul the missionary and the lessons we may learn from him today in taking the gospel to all the world. But no book on Paul would be complete without a comment, however brief, on Paul the man. And I would feel personally unsatisfied with this effort were I not to express my own love and fascination with this complicated and compelling man.

As a young missionary, I developed a deep love of the scriptures, particularly the New Testament. I smuggled into my British mission the writings of J. Reuben Clark, Jr., on the early Church, his harmony of the Gospels, and his essays on the Master. I devoured scripture commentaries and other writings by Farrar and Talmage, Hugh Nibley and Barker, Hastings, William Smith, Dummelow, Conybeare and Howson, and later C.S. Lewis, Bonhoeffer, Kierkegaard, and Tolkien.

Of course the teachings of the Master himself are the ultimate in divine teaching, unequalled by the greatest of those special witnesses who gave their testimonies of him and of his gospel. No epistle, canonical or modern, can compare with the beauty and the depth of the Sermon on the Mount, the ordination sermon given to the Twelve, or the other teachings given in the great Galilean ministry, the Judean and Perean ministries, the parables and the miracles, the intercessory prayer, the post-resurrection ministry.

But though we are given the injunction to be perfect as the Father and the Son are perfect, it is nonetheless difficult to compare oneself to Deity. It is possible for me, however, while recognizing painfully the difficulties which distinguish me from him, to identify with and hopefully try to emulate in some small way one who has come to influence my life profoundly: the apostle Paul.

Some people will for various reasons cause our spirits to vibrate more than others. I remember President David O. McKay often referring to his "favorite," the great apostle and leader of the early Church, Peter. For me, however, Paul speaks to my soul as does no other save the Master himself.

Much about Paul that is central to this volume is also central to my appreciation of the man. He, more than any other (save the Master himself), saw the universality of the Christian message. The humanity within Paul that saw the limitations of legalism must appeal to those who sense the brittleness of their own secular pharisaical age.

But other Pauline virtues, not developed in the body of this book, are nevertheless central to his attraction for me.

Paul's call for Christian charity or love provides the trumpet with certain sound in the building battle against the utter selfishness of our age of material narcissism. Nowhere better than in the writings of Paul is the battle line more clearly drawn, the competing forces better described.

On one side are the children of light: those who long for the heavenly city, the City of God, Zion. Paul taught that all of the early prophets—Abel, Enoch, Noah, Abraham, and Moses—had ultimate fidelity not to an earthly country because they "desire a better country, that is, an heavenly" where God "hath prepared for them a city" on Mount Zion, "the city of the living God, the heavenly Jerusalem." (Hebrews 11:14-16; 12:22-23.) Consequently, Saints have on earth "no continuing city, but we seek one to come." (Hebrews 13:14.) Camelot or Utopia are but secular versions of the ultimate theocratic paradigm—Zion—the perfect society without blemish, where the Saints live in righteousness, of one heart and one mind, with no poor among them; where Christ reigns and the pure in heart dwell.

On the other side of the battle line are the children of the Dark Power, who are working to build Babylon, where selfishness and a narcissistic self-love, incapable of fulfillment, prevails. Paul taught that an idolatrous, lustful covetousness of the world's wealth was the base of Babylon. "The love of money," he wrote in pastoral charge to Timothy, "is the root of all evil." (1 Timothy 6:10.)

It is perhaps no accident that a most popular form of literature of our time is a particular sort of fairy tale—of Charles Williams, C.S. Lewis's Narnia, and J.R.R. Tolkien's Middle Earth. It is in the fairy tale or myth, the myth with a golden core of insight or truth, that the reality of our time is best seen. Here the ultimate contrast between two ways, two forces—of Light and of Darkness—are developed by men of spiritual insight and are received by many who sense its truth, however unfashionable this scriptural and prophetic message may be.

Paul described the ultimate commitment of the Christian Saint to Zion, to the heavenly city, the City of God. That city had particular meaning to the Hebrews about to be faced with the destruction of the Holy City, Jerusalem. And St. Augustine understood those words as he saw in old age the beginning destruction of the Roman empire and his world in North Africa.

Paul described the antagonists of our probation in mortality:

> Be ye therefore followers of God, as dear children; . . .
> For ye were sometimes darkness, but now are ye light in the Lord: walk as children of light: . . .
> For we wrestle not against flesh and blood, but against principalities, against powers, against the rulers of the darkness of this world, against spiritual wickedness in high places.
> Wherefore take unto you the whole armour of God. (Ephesians 5:1-8; 6:12-13.)

Paul understood well the purpose of earth life. The big picture revealed the forces of Light pitted against the forces of Darkness. He warned in almost every epistle, and particularly in his pastoral letters, that the time was short, that the forces of Darkness were threatening to engulf the Church. The time of the anti-Christ was at hand. Before the Christ should come again the "man of sin" would be revealed, the "son of perdition"; the "mystery of iniquity" was already working, furthered by those who did "the working of Satan with all power and signs and lying wonders." The brethren were advised to "stand fast, and hold the traditions" that they had been taught. (See 2 Thessalonians 2.)

Timothy was told that "in the latter times" some would "depart from the faith" and be influenced by "seducing spirits, and doctrines of devils." (1 Timothy 4:1.) He was to "flee these things" and "fight the good fight of faith" that he might "lay hold on eternal life." (1 Timothy 6:11-12.)

Timothy was also cautioned to "hold fast the form of sound words" that he had heard from Paul (2 Timothy 1:13), because "perilous times" would come in the last days. Our narcissistic time of utter selfishness, the accumulation of worldly wealth at the expense of our brothers and sisters, was seen and warned against: for "men shall be lovers of their own selves." They would be "covetous," "boasters," "proud," "unthankful," and "blasphemers." They would be "lovers of pleasure more than lovers of God." And things would not improve: for "evil men and seducers shall wax worse and worse, deceiving, and being deceived."

The Christian Saint would overcome the world only by not being part of it. He could expect persecution as his Master before him. The world would not know the disciple as it had not known the Master: "all that will live godly in Christ Jesus shall suffer persecution." (2 Timothy 3:1-13.)

But Paul recognized that the Dark Power thus unwittingly fulfilled the eternal plan that had existed from the beginning. Unlike the teachings of some after the fourth century who saw the existence of evil upon the earth as a gigantic mistake, Paul understood the role of opposition, even if that role was not intended by those who initiated it. The second advent of the Master would see Babylon defeated and the forces of light triumphant. And in the meantime, the persecution, temptation, and abrasion that the world inflicted upon the Saints would make the Saints strong. For "we glory in tribulations," because "tribulation worketh patience; and patience, experience." (Romans 5:3-4.) The Lord told Joseph in

Liberty Jail that all his tribulation would work for his good. "And if thou . . . be cast into the pit; . . . if fierce winds become thine enemy; if the heavens gather blackness, . . . if the very jaws of hell shall gape open the mouth wide after thee, know thou, my son, that all these things shall give thee experience, and shall be for thy good. The Son of Man hath descended below them all. Art thou greater than he?" (D&C 122:7-8.) Just as Joseph Smith was assured that the "bounds" of opposition were "set"—"thy days are known, and thy years shall not be numbered less" (D&C 122:9)—so Paul was assured that the parameters of our earth life were beyond Satan's power.

Joseph was told: "Fear not what man can do, for God shall be with you forever and ever." (D&C 122:9.) Paul was repeatedly assured in jail, in persecutions, and in shipwreck that his life would be preserved until the completion of his life's mission.

That our mortal estate was a time of probation, of testing, of trial, and of growth was seen by Paul just as it was by Lehi, Jacob, Mormon, and Alma. Paul taught the Corinthian Saints:

> Blessed be God, even the Father of our Lord Jesus Christ, . . . the God of all comfort;
> Who comforteth us in all our tribulation. . . .
> For as the sufferings of Christ abound in us, so our consolation also aboundeth by Christ.
> And whether we be afflicted, it is for your consolation and salvation, which is effectual in the enduring of the same sufferings which we also suffer: or whether we be comforted, it is for your consolation and salvation. (2 Corinthians 1:3-6.)

If Paul understood the macrocosm—the struggle between the forces of Light and the forces of Darkness, Zion versus Babylon—he also saw the microcosm. Paul understood, before Freud, at least some of the timeless, mighty forces that exist in every soul, beneath the level of consciousness and seemingly only partially controllable by conscious sensibilities. He recognized our dependence upon repentance—a turning toward God—as the only way into the kingdom of God: as we try repeatedly to overcome forces within us, to separate out the dross from our souls. And he understood our dependence upon the guidance and support of the Spirit, who whispers to us the eternal truths we knew before but now recognize only through a glass darkly. Such truths are increasingly familiar insofar as we bring our spirits into harmony with the Holy Spirit and spiritual things, but are foolishness to the worldly. Finally, he understood our ultimate dependence upon the grace of an Atoning One:

For we know that the law is spiritual: but I am carnal, sold under sin.

For that which I do I allow not: for what I would, that do I not; but what I hate, that do I. . . .

For the good that I would I do not: but the evil which I would not, that I do. . . .

I find then a law, that, when I would do good, evil is present with me.

For I delight in the law of God after the inward man:

But I see another law in my members, warring against the law of my mind, and bringing me into captivity to the law of sin which is in my members.

O wretched man that I am! who shall deliver me from the body of this death?

I thank God through Jesus Christ our Lord. So then with the mind I myself serve the law of God; but with the flesh the law of sin. . . .

But ye are not in the flesh, but in the Spirit, if so be that the Spirit of God dwell in you. . . .

For if ye live after the flesh, ye shall die: but if ye through the Spirit do mortify the deeds of the body, ye shall live.

For as many as are led by the Spirit of God, they are the sons of God. . . .

The Spirit itself beareth witness with our spirit, that we are the children of God: . . .

For we know that the whole creation groaneth and travaileth in pain together until now.

And not only they, but ourselves also, which have the firstfruits of the Spirit, even we ourselves groan within ourselves, waiting for the adoption, to wit, the redemption of our body. . . .

Likewise the Spirit also helpeth our infirmities: for we know not what we should pray for as we ought: but the Spirit itself maketh intercession for us with groanings which cannot be uttered. (Romans 7:14-8:26.)

Paul taught that one must resist evil with all the mind and the heart. But he gave poignant and refreshingly candid testimony to the power of the flesh and the limits of the "natural man" to follow his spiritual inclinations: "For that which I do I allow not: for what I would, that do I not; but what I hate, that do I." (Romans 7:15.) Who could not identify with and appreciate this honest man? He knew that the light and the dark forces of the world were present as well in the human soul. And he recognized the limits of the ra-

7

tional, conscious ego to combat all of the powerful impulses swirling within us, encouraging us toward the satisfaction of every physical appetite and toward the mental enjoyment of pride and narcissistic self-love as well.

Paul understood that our eternal spirits are like that of our Father, and that an eternal law of growth will impel us into a greater likeness of him insofar as our prideful egos and our physical desires do not impede this growth. Often these factors so obscure our spiritual intuition that we cannot find the way. Then not only do the more sensitive spiritual parts of our souls "groan within ourselves," but also the Spirit "helpeth our infirmities." Our internal spiritual gyroscope is impeded and confused by the pride of our rational egos and the appetites of our bodies, yet it vibrates to the Holy Spirit, who gives us guidance even though our rational and physical selves are not perceptive: "For we know not what we should pray for as we ought: but the Spirit itself maketh intercession for us with groanings which cannot be uttered." (Romans 8:23, 26.)

Our rational selves alone, Paul taught, are insufficient at best and a deterrent on occasion. Only when our spiritual capacity provides the unerring discernment of the Spirit can we maintain spiritual equilibrium in life. For "the world by wisdom knew not God," and the "foolishness of God is wiser than men." (1 Corinthians 1:21, 25.) Men's eyes and ears cannot perceive what "God hath prepared for them that love him." God reveals such things only "by his Spirit: for the Spirit searcheth all things, yea, the deep things of God." As Christians we need not walk by the spirit of the world because

we have received . . . the spirit which is of God; that we might know the things that are freely given to us of God.

Which things also we speak, not in the words which man's wisdom teacheth, but which the Holy Ghost teacheth; comparing spiritual things with spiritual.

But the natural man receiveth not the things of the Spirit of God: for they are foolishness unto him: neither can he know them, because they are spiritually discerned. (1 Corinthians 2:9-14.)

The Lord told Joseph Smith:

Paul the Man

The word of the Lord is truth, and whatsoever is truth is light, and whatsoever is light is Spirit, even the Spirit of Jesus Christ.

And the Spirit giveth light to every man that cometh into the world; and the Spirit enlighteneth every man through the world, that hearkeneth to the voice of the Spirit. (D&C 84:45-46.)

Further, the light of Christ enlightens our eyes and quickens our understandings. (D&C 88:11.) If our eyes are single to his glory, our "whole bodies shall be filled with light, and there shall be no darkness in [us]; and that body which is filled with light comprehendeth all things." (D&C 88:67.)

Paul understood the essential nature of our eyes being single to God's glory. It is hard for me to think of any life, save One, which better represents that principle of absolute devotion, unwavering discipleship. Through persecution, stripes, shipwreck, imprisonment, and martyrdom, he kept the faith, fought a good fight, and finished the course. But he knew that the glory was God's. For if the honor and the glory weren't God's, the corrupting nature of power and pride of the rational ego would obscure the vision of the inner spiritual self. Paul knew that the inclination of the "natural man" to take credit even for the temporary overcoming of sin would result in a reassertion of the ego and the appetites, "bringing me into captivity to the law of sin which is in my members." (Romans 7:23.) The honor and glory are given the Father because only he can handle such inherently corrosive material without corruption. It is the natural inclination, Joseph taught, to be corrupted by pride, ambition, or power. (See D&C 121:34-46.) Perhaps this is part of the meaning of the Master that we must lose our life to find it.

As we concentrate with an eye single to the glory of God, the conscious mind stills. We think only of the immediate goal before us, without preoccupation even with our own sins. We overcome the natural man not by direct combat. We are taught rather to flee evil. Anyone who has done battle with the deadly force of habit has come to recognize the necessity of simply developing a new habit to meet more positively the needs that the undesirable habit was fulfilling, at least in some degree. The command to keep an eye single to God's glory is pervasive in the gospel. Witness the Master's instructions that we love God with *all* our heart, might, mind, and

9

strength; that we become *one* with the Father and the Son just as they are one with each other; that to be worthy of him we be willing to forsake father and mother; that the dead must bury the dead; that we find our life by losing it; that the light of the body is the eye, and if the eye *is single*, the whole body will be full of light. With such directions, we need not be any more concerned about the morrow than the lilies of the field. The evils of the day are sufficient for our concern, and on that level, without anticipating the future or feeling guilty for the past, they may be overcome.

This, in part, must be why Paul considered the major attributes of personality to be spiritual "gifts." (See 1 Corinthians 12 and 13.) What would superficially seem to be personality attributes to be developed, or "earned" by our own efforts, with the taking to ourselves the glory for such attainment, Paul attributed as God's spiritual gifts to us. If we took credit to ourselves for our faith, our hope, our charity, or our love, the power of pride would drive out those very attributes.

Paul knew that the refining of "the natural man" often required the refiner's fire. He understood through insight gained by personal experience the role of pain in the fulfillment of the mortal probation. He had experienced a divine revelation of the ultimate nature of our glorified state and of our heavenly city. He was "encumbered" with some kind of affliction, the removal of which he prayed for repeatedly. Finally he perceived the relation between suffering and growth:

> And lest I should be exalted above measure through the abundance of the revelations, there was given to me a thorn in the flesh, the messenger of Satan to buffet me, lest I should be exalted above measure.
>
> For this thing I besought the Lord thrice, that it might depart from me.
>
> And he said unto me, My grace is sufficient for thee: for my strength is made perfect in weakness. Most gladly therefore will I rather glory in my infirmities, that the power of Christ may rest upon me.
>
> Therefore I take pleasure in infirmities, in reproaches, in necessities, in persecutions, in distresses for Christ's sake: for when I am weak, then am I strong. (2 Corinthians 12:7-10.)

Finally, Paul perceived that we would need to improve our lives by a continual attempt to repent—to turn toward God. Our repentance, he taught, is based no less upon the atonement than is the resurrection. The latter is an automatic aspect of the atonement. Adamic sin and physical death are overcome by Christ's atonement: "As by the offense of one judgment came upon all men . . . even so by the righteousness of one the free gift came upon all men unto justification of life." (Romans 5:18.) "For as in Adam all die, even so in Christ shall all be made alive." (1 Corinthians 15:22.) But though repentance is a lifelong process whereby we "work out [our] own salvation with fear and trembling" (Philemon 2:12), it is no less efficacious than the resurrection, because of Christ's gift of the atonement. Without that gift, no amount of penitence would accomplish our salvation. No moral or ceremonial act can redeem us from sin without the Master's atonement with God the Father on our behalf. And if we considered it otherwise, giving ourselves the glory and the power for our own moral rejuvenation, perfection would elude us and pride ensnare us. For we have no medium of exchange to offer in return for Christ's act: grace "is not of him that willeth, nor of him that runneth, but of God that sheweth mercy." (Romans 9:16.) The grace of Christ extends from the resurrection unto life to the quality of life we will enjoy, through repentance, until we reach "the measure of the stature of the fulness of Christ." (Ephesians 4:13.)

"For I am persuaded, that neither death, nor life, nor angels, nor principalities, nor powers, nor things present, nor things to come, Nor height, nor depth, nor any other creature, shall be able to separate us from the love of God, which is in Christ Jesus our Lord." (Romans 8:38-39.)

One final and most important concept must be considered here. Perhaps the greatest of many legacies given Christianity by Judaism was the understanding that God was not the arbitrary, capricious, and duplicitous person that Greek and Roman pagan literature portrayed. God is our Father; he is just; he loves us as a Father. Capriciousness, duplicity, and arbitrariness are the antitheses of his nature.

From these ideas it must follow that if the final injunction of the Master is to be taken literally—that we must "go unto all nations," baptizing or teaching "every kindred and tongue, and people"—

then surely the Father must have a plan for those who had no opportunity to hear the good news in this life. The essence of Pauline universality must presuppose a missionary program for the dead as well as for the living. Otherwise God would not judge all his children by the same standard; fickleness and fortuity would replace those divine attributes of unchangeableness: the Father would be a respecter of persons, which Peter, in receiving the dramatic vision that opened the gospel to all God's children, assured us he was not.

We know by massive evidence from scripture, from the teachings of the ante-Nicene fathers, from apocryphal and pseudepigraphic literature, that the Christian Saints of the first several centuries knew of the Father's plan for salvation for the dead.

In the body of this volume, I sketch the core of the Christian gospel that Paul carried to other nations. Something as fundamental as the Christian doctrines concerning salvation for the dead—which is surely in keeping with a theme of the universal gospel being taken to *all* the Father's children, irrespective of their location in time or space—would seemingly be part of that core. But there is only one direct reference by Paul, in those epistles which have survived, to this topic. In preaching to the Saints at Corinth regarding the reality of a physical resurrection, Paul says in defense of that doctrine: "Else what shall they do which are baptized for the dead, if the dead rise not at all? why are they then baptized for the dead?" (1 Corinthians 15:29.) Since no elucidation of this doctrine was made by Paul, and since he did not refer to salvation for the dead in other surviving epistles, I do not feel justified in treating that topic as part of a Pauline "core." But since a plan of salvation for the dead would be absolutely essential if the Master's injunction of universality were to be met, and since the early Church taught such a doctrine, it must be included within any concept of a "core" gospel today. We therefore examine it here.

The early Church taught as a common and central principle that the spirit of the Master between the crucifixion and the resurrection descended into Hades, the place of the dead, to preach the gospel. There those who had not had the privilege of hearing that message while in the flesh could hear it and therefore be judged by the same judgment as those to whom the gospel was presented while they lived in mortality. Peter spoke of this in his first general epistle to the Church: "For Christ also hath once suffered for sins, the just for the unjust, that he might bring us to God, being put to death in the flesh, but quickened by the Spirit: By which also he went and preached unto the spirits in prison." (1 Peter 3:18-19.)

The Master forecast his descent into Hades (translated "hell" by the King James scholars, but denoting the place of the dead, not the domain of Satan) as he spoke to the disciples at Caesarea Philippi just prior to his transfiguration. Christ asked, "Whom do men say that I the Son of man am?" After various responses from the disciples, Peter proclaimed: "Thou art the Christ, the Son of the living God." The Savior then stated that "the gates of hell [according to the Greek, this refers to Hades, or the place of the dead] shall not prevail" against the Church. (Matthew 16:13-18.) In other words, the gates—the outer defense—of the place of the dead would not be able to prevent the gospel from entering that place and freeing those who before had been enslaved by death. Christ's atonement applied to the dead precisely as it did to the living. That plan was preached by the Son to the dead as he breached the gates of Hades between his crucifixion and resurrection.

After Christ told Peter and the disciples that "the gates of hell" (Hades) would not prevail against the Church, the Master said: "And I will give unto thee the keys of the kingdom of heaven: and whatsoever thou shalt bind on earth shall be bound in heaven: and whatsoever thou shalt loose on earth shall be loosed in heaven." (Matthew 16:19.) Joseph Smith said that Peter, James, and John received important keys and endowments upon the Mount of Transfiguration within days of the Savior's pronouncement. (HC 3:387.) This makes meaningful the Master's statement about the sealing power that affects both heaven and earth.

Tertullian, a lawyer and convert from Carthage in North Africa, writing in the second century, said: "Christ did not ascend to the higher heavens until he had descended to the lower regions, there to make the patriarchs and prophets his compotes [disciples]." (Quoted in Hugh Nibley, "Baptism for the Dead in Ancient Times," *Improvement Era*, December 1946, p. 26.)

13

The early Church knew of the Master's plan of salvation for the dead. In Peter's first general epistle he affirmed that the dead would be judged by precisely the same standards as those to whom the gospel was declared while in the flesh: "For this cause was the gospel preached also to them that are dead, that they might be judged according to men in the flesh, but live according to God in the spirit." (1 Peter 4:6.)

Clement of Alexandria, a second-century Church father, said that "the Lord descended to Hades for no other end but to preach the Gospel." (Alexander Roberts and James Donaldson, eds., *The Ante-Nicene Fathers*, vol. 2, book 6, p. 490.)

In one of the great priesthood sections of the Doctrine and Covenants, the Lord revealed to Joseph Smith that He had a plan of salvation sufficient that "not only those who believed after he came in the meridian of time, in the flesh, but all those from the beginning, even as many as were before he came, who believed in the words of the holy prophets, who spake as they were inspired by the gift of the Holy Ghost, who truly testified of him in all things, should have eternal life." (D&C 20:26.)

A remarkably similar passage is found in the writings of Irenaeus, a second-century Christian scholar, bishop of Lyons and one of the last Christians to see Polycarp, the last man known to have talked with any of the apostles, before the latter's martyrdom in A.D. 155. Even the rhythm of this inspired concept matches that given Joseph:

For it was not merely for those who believed on Him in the time of Tiberius Caesar that Christ came, nor did the Father exercise His providence for the men only who are now alive, but for all men altogether, who from the beginning, according to their capacity, in their generation have both feared and loved God, and practised justice and piety towards their neighbours, and have earnestly desired to see Christ, and to hear His voice. (Ibid., vol. 1, book 4, p. 494.)

Another remarkable similarity in early Church and restored Church inspired writing is seen in a comparison between a statement on the precise role performed by Christ in Hades as seen by Clement of Alexandria and a statement by President Joseph F. Smith. Clement said:

Wherefore the Lord preached the gospel to those in Hades. Accordingly the Scripture says, "Hades says to Destruction, 'We have not seen His form, but we have heard His voice.' ..." But how? Do not the scriptures show that the Lord preached the gospel to those that perished in the flood? ... *The apostles, following the Lord, preached the gospel to those in Hades. For it was requisite, in my opinion, that as here, so also there, the best of the disciples should be imitators of the Master*; so that He should bring to repentance those belonging to the Hebrews, and they of the Gentiles ... the Lord descended to Hades for no other end but to preach the gospel. ... It is evident that those, too, who were outside the law, having lived rightly, in consequence of the peculiar nature of the voice, though they are in Hades and in ward, on hearing the voice of the Lord, *whether that of His own person or that acting though His apostles*, with all speed turned and believed. ... And it were the exercise of no arbitrariness, for those who had departed before the advent of the Lord (not having the gospel preached to them, and having afforded no ground from themselves, in consequence of believing or not) to obtain either salvation or punishment. For it is not right that these should be condemned without trial, and that those alone who lived after the advent should have the advantage of the divine righteousness. ... If, then, He preached the gospel to those in the flesh that they might not be condemned unjustly, how is it conceivable that He did not for the same cause preach the gospel to those who had departed this life before His advent? (Clement of Alexandria, "The Miscellanies," *The Ante-Nicene Christian Library*, vol. 2 (1867), book 6, ch. 6, at pp. 329-32. Emphasis added.)

President Smith recorded that the following vision occurred on October 3, 1918, while he was studying Peter's account of Christ preaching to the spirits in prison:

As I pondered over these things ... the eyes of my understanding were opened ... and I saw the hosts of the dead. ...

While this vast multitude [of the righteous] waited and conversed, rejoicing in the hour of their deliverance ... the Son of God appeared, declaring liberty to the captives who had been faithful. And there he preached to them the ... redemption of mankind from the fall, and from individual sins on conditions of repentance. But unto the wicked he did not go, and among the ungodly and unrepentant who had defiled themselves while in the flesh, his voice was not raised, Neither did the rebellious who rejected the testimonies ... of the ancient prophets behold his presence, nor look upon his face. ...

And as I wondered ... I perceived that the Lord went not in person among the wicked and the disobedient who had rejected the truth, to teach them; But behold, from among the righteous, he organized his forces ... and commissioned them to go forth and carry the light of the gospel. ...

... our Redeemer spent his time ... in the world of spirits, instructing and preparing the faithful spirits ... who had testified of him in the flesh; That they might carry the message of redemption unto all the dead, unto whom he could not go personally, because of their rebellion and transgression. . . .

Among the great and mighty ones who were assembled in this vast congregation of the righteous were Father Adam . . . , Eve, with many of her faithful daughters, . . . Abel, . . . Seth, . . . Noah . . . , Shem . . . , Abraham . . . , Isaac, Jacob . . . , Moses . . . , Ezekiel . . . , Daniel . . . , the prophets [of] the Nephites . . . , Joseph Smith . . . , Hyrum Smith, Brigham Young [and many others]. I beheld that the faithful elders of this dispensation, when they depart from mortal life, continue their labors in the preaching of the gospel. (D&C 138:11-57.)

Origen, one of the greatest Christian theologians of all time, whose life spanned the latter part of the second century and the first half of the third century, defended Christian teachings against Celsus, a literary critic of Christianity. Celsus said: "You will not, I suppose, say of him [Jesus], that, after failing to gain over those who were in this world, he went to Hades to gain over those who were there." To this Origen replied: "We assert that not only while Jesus was in the body did He win over not a few persons; . . . but also, that when He became a soul, without the covering of the body, He dwelt among those souls which were without bodily covering, converting such of them as were willing to Himself. . . ." (Roberts and Donaldson, *The Ante-Nicene Fathers*, vol. 4, book 2, p. 448.)

While the gospel was preached and a great missionary force thus organized to preach to the dead, essential ordinances on behalf of the dead were performed by the living Saints so that those who had departed might literally "be judged according to men in the flesh, but live according to God in the spirit." (1 Peter 4:6.) It was in regard to the ordinance of baptism, vicariously performed by the living Christians on behalf of the dead, to which Paul referred in his letter to the Saints at Corinth. This ancient Christian ordinance survived, though often in perverted form, at least into the fifth century.

The Church of Jesus Christ of Latter-day Saints maintains that the sealing power committed to Peter and the apostles in an earlier era has been restored again in this time. In addition, the prophet Elijah has returned to commit other keys of salvation, in fulfillment of the prophecy of Malachi: "Behold, I will send you Elijah the prophet before the coming of the great and dreadful day of the Lord: And he shall turn the heart of the fathers to the children, and the heart of the children to their fathers, lest I come and smite the earth with a curse." (Malachi 4:5-6.)

This restoration of keys has an important impact on us. Our day is one of future shock. Change comes so rapidly that it is difficult to adjust psychologically. Our fathers had to be able to adjust to a technological revolution—and the resulting changes in political and philosophical superstructure—only once in their lifetimes, if that. Today we experience such a revolution every four years.

Our culture is on wheels—and wings. People born in Alabama may live in seven or ten locations beyond their "native" state and retire in California. National electronic media bombard us nightly with more current events than we can handle. The frustration of impotence is evident. At the same time, little history is presented us as we rely more and more upon television—a medium that recognizes no history—for our world view, rather than upon books. Our own local culture and our own past are thus forgotten or overwhelmed.

A people who forget their past cut themselves free from its continuity. We end up without a sense of history and without an internal gyroscope to guide us in our own time. The result is a state of narcissism. We are not concerned with the past or our own traditions. The curse of anomie follows—a state of normlessness in which we are "tossed to and fro, and carried about with every wind of doctrine, by the sleight of men, and cunning craftiness, whereby they lie in wait to deceive." (Ephesians 4:14.) Surely the curse of Malachi is upon us and can only be removed by a turning of the hearts of the fathers to the children and of the children to the fathers.

Abraham recorded that he kept priesthood records "for the benefit of my posterity." (Abraham 1:31.)

Nephite prophets sensed the necessity of their own genealogy and their own records as they left their own Near Eastern culture and traveled under God's direction to a new, wild, and unsettled continent. The early parts of the Book of Mormon might well be characterized as the "saga of the Plates of Laban." The ancient record that Lehi's family brought with them helped that branch of Israel maintain the language, the culture, and the religion of their fathers. The prophets among them constantly used the plates to teach of the heritage of their people. Especially during the crisis of the second generation—those who could not remember the "land of Jerusalem"—the records were relied upon in order to connect a dangerously rootless generation with their past.

"You are of Israel!" their prophets repeated again and again, and incorporated into their own records the prophecies of Isaiah, which emphasized the promises of Jehovah to Israel.

Nephi recorded that "we labor diligently to write, to persuade our children . . . to believe in Christ, and to be reconciled to God." (2 Nephi 25:23.) The Mulekite people, migrating to a new world without bringing written records, lost a written language over time and disintegrated as a people. Nephi was told that his people would "dwindle and perish in unbelief" without a record of their fathers. (1 Nephi 4:13.) King Benjamin told his sons that "were it not for these things [the written records of their people] which have been kept and preserved by the hand of God, that we might read and understand . . . even our fathers would have dwindled in unbelief." (Mosiah 1:5.)

The Lord directed his Church on the very day of its organization in this dispensation that "there shall be a record kept among you." (D&C 21:1.)

We have been instructed to keep personal journals today that we might link our children to their fathers and ourselves to our fathers. Thus we maintain a rudder to guide us through life and avoid the curse of rootlessness of our age.

It is to accomplish the same purposes that we today turn our hearts to the fathers—in the vicarious performance of saving ordinances, in discovering our own taproots of genealogy. For this purpose we build temples. Paul taught that those who have departed this life need our help: that "they without us should not be made perfect." (Hebrews 11:40.) But surely we cannot avoid the curse of rootlessness and anomie without them.

This final arena of missionary activity in a sense is the epitome of the Pauline example. The gospel of the Master is thus presented back and forth between the living and the dead as a universal statement of love expressed in both directions through the veil, across the expanse of space and time, the pure in heart linking Zion and the temple together, the gates of Hades shattered.

This book about the apostle Paul is not a scholarly treatise on his life and letters. That has been done by others better equipped, such as the classical studies of Farrar, Conybeare and Howson, and David Smith, though those sources have been read and relied upon for their original research. Rather, we here examine Paul's life and his writings in the context of taking the gospel to the entire world.

Paul was the great apostle to the gentile world and the greatest missionary the Christian faith has ever known. He was the chosen vessel of the Lord to carry his gospel between people of different lands and cultures.

Today we are faced with the responsibility of preaching the gospel of Jesus Christ to all the nations of the earth, which have been brought closer in some ways by modern technology. But that technology—the transistor radio, worldwide television by satellite, supersonic planes and missiles—has not homogenized the Father's children. And closeness can produce abrasion as well as affection. The people of the nations remain startlingly and delightfully diverse.

Of course, forced regimentation and uniformity of culture are no solution for those who believe in the eternal and uncreated individuality of every soul. But the idiosyncracies of individuals and the cultural chasms separating countries provide great challenge to those who would preach and those who would listen.

The key of Christian charity, or love, was both demonstrated and written about by Paul as clearly as by anyone who has ever lived, save One. Paul's life and letters are here examined in an attempt better to understand how an eternal and universal gospel may best be preached by and to people limited by time and place.

Chapter Two

The Challenge: "Teach All Nations"

The parting commission of the resurrected Lord to the Twelve and to the Church was that they were to be witnesses of him not only in Jerusalem, in Judea, and in Samaria, but "unto the uttermost part of the earth," to "go . . . into all the world" and "teach all nations, baptizing them in the name of the Father, and of the Son, and of the Holy Ghost." (Acts 1:8; Mark 16:15; Matthew 28:29.)

This awesome yet joyous burden of teaching and bearing witness to all nations assumes that there is a gospel message of universal applicability. That is, the enormous cultural differences that separate humankind apparently do not preclude the preaching of the gospel of the Master to "every nation, and kindred, and tongue, and people." (D&C 133:37.) Those same social filters that may estrange the Father's children on so many other bases need not prevent the reception of that gospel by anyone.

Further, since the injunction of the Lord could not be accomplished in one generation, or indeed one century or millennium, it must follow that the gospel of the kingdom is not only universal in space (i.e., applicable to the people of the Middle Eastern cultural home of Jesus, and in Asia, Europe, and Africa, America and the islands), but that the gospel is universal in time as well. It loses no relevance in twentieth-century culture even though it was presented millennia ago. The gospel, then, is to be preached to people of every culture, place, and time.

Finally, since we know that the Lord gives no commandment without preparing a way for its accomplishment, we know that those political barriers which now preclude gospel preaching in some lands will be breached by the Lord when we have prepared ourselves to enter. In this dispensation, the Lord has directed his assurance to the First Presidency and the Twelve: "Whosoever ye shall send in my name, by the voice of your brethren, the Twelve, duly recommended and authorized by you, shall have power to open the door of my kingdom unto any nation whithersoever ye shall send them." (D&C 112:21.)

But the practical problems are enormous. The natural tendency of the missionary may be to include much of his own culture in the gospel message he attempts to convey to people of another culture. Our thought processes, symbols, and means of communication are all affected by our culture. And those who hear the gospel message are similarly conditioned by their culture.

How then can a universal message of an Eternal Father be preached across cultures?

This seeming paradox of preaching a perfect and universal message through and to imperfect and very different people is made more complex in a sense by one of the unique teachings of Mormon theology. We believe that the gospel was not first introduced to this earth by the Master in the meridian of time. Rather, the Father's plan was presented to his children before the earth's creation. Thereafter, the gospel was preached to Adam. Jesus as Jehovah preached the same gospel to Abraham and to Moses. It has been upon the earth, through different dispensations and in various degrees of completeness, from that time to this. It has existed within governments as simple as Lehi's patriarchal community and as complex as the Roman imperial system. It has flowered under governments that have allowed freedom of worship and expression and insured order; it has survived and grown under tyrannical and corrupt governments.

Apart from the governmental differences of host countries, Christianity has grown in vastly different societies as well, and these sociological differences are often more striking and difficult to adjust to than are differences in governmental form. It has fit into simple Bedouin desert communities and into the great cities of the world. The gospel was presented by the Master during his ministry to a Middle Eastern Jewish community. But, largely due to the ministry of Paul, the gospel took root in Asia Minor and in Europe as well.

Nor is it meant that Christ's message should be inextricably linked to the governmental or social mores or customs of any particular community, be it Palestine or the United States or Western Europe or whatever. Neither political and economic structure nor social customs of particular areas should be attached to the core of Christ's gospel, because to do so would be to add a limiting element to a timeless and universal message. Political forms from the Greek city state to Western democratic parliamentary government arise because of peculiar social conditions and are modified or disappear as these conditions change. Other social mores and customs are native to certain parts of America, Europe, Africa, or Asia.

We must learn to distinguish between the timeless and universal gospel of the Master and the politics and the sociology of a particular time and place. Not to do so would be to link an eternal message with political and social institutions, which contain within themselves the seeds of their own death; such institutions have a life expectancy directly related to the time and circumstance of their creation.

And if particular political and social forms are attached to the gospel, it will be difficult and in some situations impossible to carry such a message, thus made unnecessarily alien to different political and cultural traditions, to other parts of the world. The Master's final injunction to the Twelve to carry the gospel to all nations could not be met.

This does not mean, of course, that political and social factors will not or should not influence, to some degree, the nature of our forms of worship in our own particular community. Indeed, it is probably impossible that pure gospel principles could be isolated in their application from the social conditions of our lives, since we have no alternative but to attempt to apply those principles within the social matrix of our own time and place. Only symbols natural to our own situation may be sufficiently powerful to motivate us to apply the gospel in our lives.

But we must, by intense spiritual and intellectual efforts, still learn to distinguish between pure gospel principles and our own politics and sociology. This is probably necessary for our own spiritual growth, and it is essential to our ability to export the gospel to different lands and cultures. The gospel message that is taken to other lands, if it is to be accepted, must be shorn of those political and social accretions of the exporting state in order that it not be alien to the receiving culture. Only the universal message of the Master can be carried to all parts of the world and there take natural root and be accepted.

In these receiving lands, quite naturally, we must allow the members of the Church the same liberty of worship that we enjoy; we must expect local political and social elements to influence the nature of their worship service, to a certain degree.

Governments will allow different levels of activity by the Church. And as long as the essential aspects of worship are allowed, the Church can function, Church literature can be distributed and used, sacraments can be performed, worship services will be condoned, assembly will be allowed, and individual worship will be permitted, if not encouraged. The minimum, though far from ideal, is sufficient.

While the universal gospel of Jesus Christ will be preached in every land, inevitably there will be local forms of worship determined by the nature of the society. Social customs will determine that different images and symbols will be used. The art, architecture, musical forms and instruments, food, clothing style, literature, dance, symbolism, and ritual of the local society will all dictate variations in approaches to worship. "For behold, the Lord doth grant unto all nations, of their own nation and tongue, to teach his word, yea, in wisdom, all that he seeth fit that they should have." (Alma 29:8.) For "every man shall hear the fulness of the gospel in his own tongue, and in his own language." (D&C 90:11.)

The gospel message preached in Provo, Utah, will be the same as that preached in Warsaw, Poland, or in Accra, Ghana, but the conditions of its preachment and the manifestations of its practice will differ. Through Nephi, the Lord reminds us that he is concerned about *all* nations: "Know ye not that there are more nations than one? Know ye not that I, the Lord your God, have created all men, and that I remember those who are upon the isles of the sea; and that I rule in the heavens above and in the earth beneath; and I bring forth my word unto the children of men, yea, even upon all the nations of the earth?" (2 Nephi 29:7.)

A Ptolemaic universe, in a national and cultural sense, must not be imposed on the propagation of the gospel, with other cultures revolving around our own. For "Zion must increase in beauty, and in holiness; her borders must be enlarged; her stakes must be strengthened." (D&C 82:14.) And this demands a proper regard for the governmental form and the cultural traditions of every people.

The eventual failure of the early church to discriminate between the universal gospel and elements of pagan superstition and Roman imperial political structure led eventually to apostasy. The seeds of death implicit in the Roman Empire infected the church as the latter came to mirror the former. Church government came to be fashioned on the Roman imperial model rather than upon the apostolic model of the first century. And gospel teachings came to be influenced substantially by the pagan cultures in which they were preached.

The result was disastrous. The church began to demand rigid conformity on the social and cultural levels. The great advantage of Christianity of the first century, its universalism without inextricable attachment to a particular social order, was lost as the church of the fourth century demanded that host countries and peoples accept the Roman and later Byzantine imperial structure and Latin and Greek forms. The refusal of the church during these times to allow local social and political institutions to play their natural roles left it rootless in some foreign lands. In the eighth century Islam swept aside these rootless forms of Christianity from much of Asia Minor, North Africa, Spain, and the Middle East. The politics and the sociology of both Rome and Constantinople were alien to these cultures. The necessity of scriptures in the local vernacular and music, ritual, and teachings presented in ways in harmony with local society is apparent.[1]

Similarly in some respects, by the Middle Ages and the rise of modern nationalism, the export of Christianity to Asia and Africa was intermixed with nationalistic conquest and cultural domination. Seemingly promising Christian missions to Asia and Africa in the fourteenth century had all but disappeared by the sixteenth. Attempts by the exporting states to demand alien political and social forms and ideas, intermixed indiscriminately with gospel teachings, not only corrupted the message but ensured that local customs, no matter how compatible with the universal "core" of Christianity, would have to be rejected as the price of Christian membership. This left the local Christian community alien, rootless, impotent, and vulnerable to a competing religion with a base in natural harmony with the local culture.

By contrast, the church of the first century preached a universal gospel that allowed some local political and cultural variations in worship—though certainly not in doctrine. The approach of the early church serves as our great model. The church of the first century carried the gospel from its people and land of origin, the Jewish Christian community, to the gentile world of the Mediterranean countries from Palestine and Syria to Asia Minor, European Greece and Rome, and North Africa. And the central figure in that early missionary effort was the great apostle to the gentiles, Paul.

---

[1]The remarkable resilience of Coptic Christianity is a tribute to its universality and to its deeply rooted base in harmony with the local cultures. See Aziz Atiya, *History of Eastern Christianity* and *The Copts and Christian Civilization*, cited in the Bibliography.

Chapter Three

The Palestine of Saul

Paul was born Saul (his Jewish name), of Jewish parents residing in Tarsus, a gentile city. That Saul's early years were spent among Jews of the dispersion and gentiles may have helped nurture his universality of spirit, which was to be so critical to that purpose for which the Lord was preparing him from the beginning. Saul was born a Roman citizen and, in the footsteps of his father, was trained a Pharisee. He was proficient in Greek and Hebrew and continued his education at Jerusalem, probably in his middle teens, learning the law at the feet of Gamaliel, probably grandson of Hillel and the same master of the law to whom the honored title "Rabban" was given. As was the Jewish custom, he also learned a trade as tentmaker.

Palestine of Saul's day was powerfully influenced by the Greek and Roman presence and by the Jewish reaction to it. The Hellenistic culture of the Greek world of Alexander had pervaded the Mediterranean world three hundred years before Saul and was by far the dominant cultural influence still. The Roman governance and law combined with the Greek culture to threaten the weaker Jewish culture with obliteration, either by outright destruction or elimination by assimilation.

Two hundred years before Christ, this fight for survival of

Jewish culture in a Greco-Roman sea had split Jewish leadership into two camps. The Sadducees sought accommodation with Greek culture by assimilating much of its philosophy into Judaism and by collaborating closely with Roman governance. The Pharisees considered this to be cultural suicide, but their response in the opposite direction was so reactionary that they perverted the humane, compassionate, and tender Mosaic law into sterile legalism. The Pharisees elaborated the law until the people became its slaves, straining at every gnat of detail and overlooking its weightier morality.

This condition of Palestine and Judaism, suffering cultural onslaught from a far more sophisticated Greek philosophy and dominated by Roman rule, led directly to those problems that Saul as Paul was to confront as the great Apostle to the Gentiles.

The gospel, of course, was originally preached exclusively to the Jews. Early Christianity was not seen as being antithetical to continued temple worship and Jewish orthodoxy. The early Church enjoyed substantial growth from among Pharisees, due in part to the fact that both groups believed the doctrine of the resurrection. But when gentile conversions began to occur, critical decisions had to be made. Must the gentile convert become Christian by first becoming a Jewish proselyte? Must the Jewish ceremonial law, including circumcision, be demanded of the gentile convert? Granted that the Jewish Christian saw no incompatibility with his Jewish and his Christian religion and worshipped both at the temple and synagogue and within his Christian community, was the same to be a prerequisite for the gentile convert's new life as a Christian? Conservative or Pharisaical Christians quite naturally saw any retreat from "Jewishness" as another threat to their embattled culture, leading to assimilation into the Greco-Roman world. Yet to demand complete fidelity to Jewish ceremonial law on the part of the gentile converts would limit the infant Christian faith to a future no more universal than that of just another of the many Jewish sects.

Paul's response to this crisis would at once lead to implacable opposition from Pharisaical Christianity that would last throughout his ministry, serve as his greatest contribution to the propagation of the faith of his Master, undoubtedly cause him more personal grief than any other event in his life as one misunderstood and rejected by his own, lead ultimately and directly to his death, and ensure his monument as the servant through whom the Lord caused his gospel to be preached beyond Palestine and Asia Minor to Europe and the larger gentile world.

The work of the greatest missionary the world has ever known was preceded by that of two valiant forerunners, Stephen and Philip, who in a sense filled a preparatory role similar to that accomplished by John the Baptist.

Stephen preached a universal gospel that cost the fledgling Christian community at Jerusalem much of its Pharisaical support. Stephen's preaching was seen as a threat to Jewish cultural purity and left the Christian community vulnerable to persecution from its right flank, heretofore protected by the Pharisees. The persecution resulted in Stephen's death and, ironically, probably led directly to Christians fleeing Jerusalem for outer regions such as Syrian Antioch, where a gentile Christian community evolved, apparently without any conscious decision being made regarding the property and requirements of gentile Church membership. It is possible that the foundation of the Christian community at Rome itself stemmed from this first general Jewish persecution and the consequent flight of the Christians from Jerusalem.

Philip performed the role of honored forerunner to the Apostle to the Gentiles by doing two important things. First, he preached to the Samaritans, who were not exactly Jewish and not exactly gentile; it was a half-step toward openly proselytizing the gentile world. Peter and John placed their stamp of approval on these acts by bestowing the Holy Ghost upon Philip's Samaritan converts. Second, he taught and baptized the Ethiopian eunuch, who was familiar and sympathetic with the Jewish scripture and worship, but was not a Jew.

But the profound exclusivity of the Jewish people, fostered by divine law, ran deep. It was hard, almost impossible, for the people to conceive that much of that law was to endure for a time as a schoolmaster rather than to be an end in itself. And the law established both religious and social distinctions, each reinforcing the other, between the Jews and the gentile world. The idolatry and immorality of the pagan world were repugnant to Jewry. National isolation was maintained even by Jews of the dispersion; for example, the law forbade eating with gentiles. It even restricted Jews from eating many gentile foods.

Knowing how powerfully the law held the Jews, the Lord used the images of food and eating in a vision that was to open the door for the gospel to go to all nations. In the vision, Peter beheld as a "certain vessel" descended from heaven, containing forms of food forbidden by the law. He was commanded to eat. He responded, "Not so, Lord; for I have never eaten any thing that is common or unclean." The answer from heaven would lead to the greatest revolution the world had ever known, as Christianity was made universal: "What God hath cleansed, that call not thou common." (Acts 10:9-16.)

Peter understood the application of these instructions when Cornelius, a devout gentile centurion, approached and reported his own vision: an angel instructed Cornelius, the gentile, to go to Peter, the Jewish Christian, for salvation.

Peter's vision taught that salvation comes directly through Jesus Christ. He is the way, and no prerequisite of Jewishness or Jewish ceremonial law was to interdict the path of conversion and the gate of baptism and full fellowship in the Christian community.

A general principle can be seen within this specific and crucial event in Christian history. A person need not fulfill any prerequisite related to nationality or peculiar social custom before he can be baptized into full Christian fellowship. Baptism is conditioned only upon belief in Jesus Christ and a willingness to abide his teachings.

With Peter's vision the stage was set for the fulfillment of the Master's final injunction: to carry his gospel to every nation.

Chapter Four

The Apostle to the Gentiles

With the irony that so often marks the advancement of Christ's gospel, the tragedy of the first Christian martyrdom, the death of Stephen, eventually spread Christianity throughout the body of the Roman Empire. With the increasing persecution, Christians fled to Antioch and to Damascus, and most probably to Rome itself. Saul, who had consented to Stephen's death and kept the clothes of those suborned witnesses who cast the first stones at Stephen, now traveled toward Damascus to wreak havoc among the followers of "the way."

Saul's conversion on the road to Damascus is one of those seminal events that changed world history. A vision of the risen Lord burst upon Saul. In response to the Master's query, "Why persecutest me?" Saul answered, "Who art thou, Lord?" He was told, "I am Jesus whom thou persecutest." (Acts 9:1-7.) From that moment Saul became God's slave. The zeal (and so much more) that had gone into the persecution of God's church now turned toward its propagation, ultimately to fill the world.

After restoration of sight and baptism by Ananias, Saul retired into Arabia for spiritual communion, better to understand his direct mandate from his Master. He preached for a time at Damascus, later visited Jerusalem and met Peter and James, "the Lord's brother," through introduction by Barnabas, and ultimately returned to Tarsus until Barnabas called him to Antioch.

The Christian dispersion from Jerusalem following Stephen's martyrdom had led to a thriving Christian community at Syrian Antioch and to the conversion of many gentiles. The Twelve at Jerusalem sent a trusted brother, Barnabas, to investigate this phenomenon, and he in turn called down Saul from Tarsus to help him evaluate the problem of gentile Christianity at Antioch. Both pronounced it good and recommended approval and support from the Twelve. Barnabas and Saul returned to Antioch following their report at Jerusalem and from there were called on their first great missionary journey to Cyprus, a major Roman senatorial province, and through Asia Minor. They preached first to the Jews of the synagogue and then (particularly at Antioch in Pisidia, after little success among the Jewish congregation) they turned to the gentiles.

On the first Sabbath at Pisidian Antioch, Saul preached to the Jews in their synagogue. They seemed to receive enthusiastically the message that Jesus was indeed the Messiah whose coming had been foretold. Then at the second Sabbath a congregation of Jews and many interested gentiles heard Saul preach a more universal message. He preached that the Messiah was more than "the glory of his people Israel"; he was "a light to lighten the Gentiles" as well. As it became evident that a majority of the Jews would reject their message, Barnabas and Saul turned from the Jews to the gentiles to form a new Israel: "For so hath the Lord commanded us, saying, I have set thee to be a light of the Gentiles, that thou shouldest be for salvation unto the ends of the earth." Paul declared: "It was necessary that the word of God should first have been spoken to you: but seeing ye put it from you, and judge yourselves unworthy of everlasting life, lo, we turn to the Gentiles." (Acts 13:46-47.) From this point in the narrative of the Acts of the Apostles, Luke records the symbolic change in the name of the apostle: the Jewish name "Saul" is replaced by the Roman "Paul"; Saul, the devout Christian Pharisee, becomes Paul, the missionary to the gentile world of the empire of Rome. He thereafter takes precedence over Barnabas in Luke's account in Acts: "Barnabas and Saul" become "Paul and Barnabas," beloved companions who were to share in a magnifi-

31

cent harvest. Branches of the Church were established at Cyprus, at Antioch in Pisidia, at Iconium, Lystra, and Derbe.

Their great success among the gentiles of Asia Minor led to the first Church council at Jerusalem, perhaps the most important event in the life of Paul, after his conversion itself. Barnabas, a Jewish Christian, and Titus, an uncircumcised Greek gentile convert to Christianity, accompanied Paul to the city of Jerusalem, which Paul had left fifteen years before, as Saul, to persecute the Christians at Damascus. They came to report phenomenal success in the baptism of thousands of gentiles. The meeting with Peter and the other apostles at Jerusalem was made necessary because "certain men" had been teaching the necessity of circumcision for the new gentile converts.

At the council, Peter spoke first. He reminded the leaders that God had informed the Church that the gentiles should hear the gospel; further, there was "no difference" between "them and us," even without the Mosaic law's ceremonial acts of purification, because God had purified "their hearts by faith. Now therefore why tempt ye God, to put a yoke upon the neck of the disciples, which neither our fathers nor we were able to bear?" (Acts 15:10.)

But it was James the Just, the "brother of the Lord" and the living symbol of traditional and conservative Jewry, who defeated the "Judaizers," those Jewish Christian Pharisees who later followed Paul on his second missionary journey, attempting to subvert the final decision of the council at Jerusalem. James declared the law to be a preparation for the Christian gospel: "Wherefore my sentence is, that we trouble not them which from among the Gentiles are turned to God." James proposed that they send an apostolic epistle, the first of which we have record, to the gentile churches at Antioch, Syria, and Cilicia with Paul, Barnabas, and two special emissaries from the Church at Jerusalem, Judas and Silas. The letters were simply to direct the gentile members to abstain from idolatry and fornication and, as a gesture to improve social relations between gentile and Jewish Christians, to abstain from "things strangled, and from blood. . . .

"For it seemed good to the Holy Ghost, and to us, to lay upon you no greater burden than these necessary things." (Acts 15:20, 28.)

Thus the decision of the council was to reinforce the principle that Christ, not Judaism, was the gate through which all must pass. Judaic ceremony, including circumcision, was not to be prerequisite to Christian membership. This shattering decision was to make possible the spread of Christianity throughout the Roman world. Paul was now to fulfill that possibility.

The second missionary journey began under a cloud as Paul refused to allow John Mark, the nephew of Barnabas and later the author of the Gospel that bears his name, to travel with them. The young Mark, who had displeased Paul by leaving him at Pamphylia during the first missionary journey, now traveled with Barnabas to Cyprus while Paul took Silas through Syria and Cilicia, retracing the first journey, strenthening the newly formed branches of the Church.

It was on the second missionary journey that the Holy Ghost moved upon Paul in such a way as again to change radically the history of the world. After he visited the churches at Galatia established during the first missionary journey, and after he was joined by Timothy at Lystra, instead of going as he had planned from Phyrgia and Galatia to other parts of Asia Minor Paul was told by the Spirit to go to Troas. In a vision Paul saw a man of Macedonia who pleaded for him to introduce the gospel there. Paul, Timothy, Luke, Silas, and others sailed from Troas to Macedonia and first preached the gospel in Europe at Philippi, a Greek city. Paul later preached at Thessalonica and at Athens, delivering the masterful sermon on Mars' Hill. He spent some time at Corinth, the most important Roman center of commerce and government in European Greece; there he probably wrote his epistle to the Thessalonians, the first of those letters which were to comprise a major part of the New Testament canon.

After their return to Jerusalem to celebrate Pentecost at the conclusion of the second missionary journey, Paul returned to Antioch. On his third missionary journey increasing conservative opposition manifested itself. Groups of Judaizers, falsely claiming authorization from James the Just, hounded Paul's footsteps, trying to reverse the decision of the council of Jerusalem that the ceremonial law need not be demanded of the new gentile Christian converts. Failing that, opponents of open and equal gentile membership attempted to create class stratification and segregation in the Church, placing gentile Christians in an inferior position. The segregation was symbolized by eating separately, as the law required Jews do with gentiles. (See Paul's rebuke to Peter for the latter's refusal to eat with Gentiles on one occasion: Galatians 2:11-16.)

Then a new problem presented itself, and Paul had to deal not only with the relationship between the Jewish law and gentile membership, but also with the crisis of paganism: in what manner can the gospel best be taken to a people alien to the Judaic matrix within which Christianity developed? And how could the apostolic leadership help prevent pagan heresies from perverting Christian teachings and yet, at the same time, ensure that the gospel would accommodate those customs of Asia Minor, Greece, and Rome that were not antithetical to the gospel? New converts to Christianity from pagan backgrounds brought with them a history of indulgence in morally dissolute and licentious activities, sometimes as a part of pagan religious ceremony. The temptation to revert to heathen immorality after a lifetime of such activity, especially when the whole social structure of the community approved such behavior, was powerful. Paul's letters to the Saints at Corinth reveal not only his deep concern for the activities of the Judaizers of Hebrew background, but also for the immorality endemic to the members of the Church at Corinth, who were predominantly gentile and pagan in background.

From approximately August of A.D. 52 until Pentecost of A.D. 56, Paul retraced most of his earlier journeys, shoring up the Christian communities he had established and strengthening his spiritual children. During his first and second missionary journeys, Paul had selected the political and commercial centers of the Roman empire in which to found the Christian churches, ensuring that by natural contact the church of God would spread throughout the empire. For just under three years on his third journey, Paul remained at Ephesus, the capital of the Roman province of Asia and the most important seaport of Asia Minor. He taught "all Asia" from this strategic headquarters. It was here that he wrote one of the most beautiful of all works of scripture, the first epistle to the Corinthians.

After leaving Ephesus, Paul traveled to Macedonia. Here, probably at Philippi, he wrote the second epistle to the Corinthians. He then went into Greece; and at Corinth he wrote the first great systematic treatise of Christian theology, the epistle to the Romans. Before reaching Ephesus, Paul had visited Galatia. Now while at Corinth he received word from Galatia that the Judaizers had mounted the most offensive and serious challenge yet to his apostleship. After suffering (as only a missionary can suffer) the Judaizers' attempts to destroy the faith of his converts, he wrote his most abrasive and, in some ways, his most powerful defense of his apostleship—an awesome attack on those who taught that salvation would come through the ceremonial law—the great epistle to the Galatians.

Paul returned to Jerusalem at the end of the third missionary journey to celebrate the Pentecost as the devout and proper Jew he was to the end of his days. Here occurred the persecution of which he had been forewarned: his imprisonment at Jerusalem; his hearing before the high priest Ananias; his imprisonment at Caesarea; his trials before Felix and Festus; his appeal as a Roman citizen to Caesar rather than face return to Jerusalem and certain death; his voyage to Rome and shipwreck; his house imprisonment at Rome and the poignant and yet politic letter to Philemon; his vibrant testimony of Christ's divinity delivered to the Colossians; his joyful letter to that branch which always remained faithful to Paul and which he never had to rebuke, the Philippians, his "dearest children of the faith." And finally, as one of the most beautiful of all epistles of the New Testament, his letter to the Ephesians. It is the most powerful statement in all scripture of the universal Christian fellowship that transcends artificial groupings of nationality or race. Like Joseph Smith's travail at Liberty Jail, Paul's travail of imprisonment gave birth to testaments of such beauty and power that one approaches them in reverence and in awe.

While the book of the Acts of the Apostles ends strangely at this point, we know with some assurance at least the outline of that which came after: Paul's release from Roman imprisonment; his missionary labors in Europe and in Asia Minor, and perhaps into Spain; his pastoral epistles to Timothy and Titus, his beloved spiritual children and missionary companions, now leaders at Ephesus and Crete; then his second imprisonment and, with death assured, his last powerful testimony to the world, the second epistle to Timothy:

> For I am now ready to be offered, and the time of my departure is at hand.
> I have fought a good fight, I have finished my course, I have kept the faith:
> Henceforth there is laid up for me a crown of righteousness, which the Lord, the righteous judge, shall give me at that day: and not to me only, but unto all them also that love his appearing. (2 Timothy 4:6-8.)

This was followed by his execution as a Roman citizen outside the walls of Rome about A.D. 67 or 68.

Chapter Five

"He Shall Teach You All Things"

One inescapable conclusion emerges from viewing the life of Paul as a paradigm for taking the gospel to every nation: the guidance of the Holy Ghost is essential. Without the Holy Spirit we are left to our own wisdom, which is a weak reed, insufficient to mark the way.

While the Father expects us to struggle in our minds, to grapple with the problems that confront us, to think, to observe past experiences such as those afforded by the world of Paul, our efforts must be interlaced with prayer. And finally the Spirit must illuminate the path. Surely this was so in the course of the early Church and in the lives of Peter and Paul.

Every critical decision made in connection with carrying the gospel to the gentiles was determined under the direction of the Holy Ghost.

While operating simply on his own determination of God's will, Saul was on the way to Damascus to persecute the Church; then the Master intervened. It is possible that before this divine intervention the Spirit was working within Saul to trouble him. Perhaps, though we can only speculate, he had been thus troubled since he witnessed the death of Stephen. The Master noted that it was "hard" for Saul to "kick against the pricks." (Acts 9:3-7.)

Peter's vision while on a housetop at Joppa provided the authoritative direction that gentile conversion was possible, acceptable, even demanded of God: "What God hath cleansed, that call not thou common." (Acts 10:9-16.) Peter sanctioned gentile baptism only after he observed that "on the Gentiles also was poured out the gift of the Holy Ghost. . . . Can any man forbid water, that these should not be baptized, which have received the Holy Ghost as well as we?" (Acts 10:45-47.)

Barnabas, sent by the brethren at Jerusalem to Syrian Antioch to observe there the phenomenon of spontaneous gentile conversion, was "a good man, and full of the Holy Ghost." (Acts 11:24.)

The Holy Ghost separated Paul and Barnabas for their first great missionary journey through Cyprus and Asia Minor.

Paul and Barnabas first determined to "turn to the Gentiles" in active proselytizing at Antioch in Pisidia as directed by the Lord: "For so hath the Lord commanded us, saying, I have set thee to be a light of the Gentiles, that thou shouldest be for salvation unto the ends of the earth." (Acts 13:46-47.)

The great council at Jerusalem reached it epochal conclusion not to require ceremonial Judaism of the gentile convert to Christianity by revelation through the Holy Ghost: "For it seemed good to the Holy Ghost, and to us, to lay upon you no greater burden than these necessary things." (Acts 15:28.)

The gospel was first taken to Europe and Asia Minor as a result of direct heavenly intervention. A "vision appeared to Paul in the night": a "man of Macedonia" appeared to him while he was in Mysia in Galatia, in Asia Minor. Paul had intended to go further in the same general area, into Bithynia in the Roman province of Asia, but he and his companions were "forbidden of the Holy Ghost to preach the word in Asia"; "the Spirit suffered them not." Paul was directed by the angelic messenger to "Come over into Macedonia, and help us." (Acts 16:6-9.) Thus the gospel was first preached in Europe as Paul and Silas established a branch of the Church at Philippi, among those whom Paul would later lovingly call his "dearest children of the faith."

Nearing the end of his ministry, Paul, under arrest in Jerusalem following his return from the third missionary journey, was told in a vision that he would bear witness yet farther west, at the very capital of the western world: "The Lord stood by him, and said, Be of good cheer, Paul: for as thou hast testified of me in Jerusalem, so must thou bear witness also at Rome." (Acts 23:11.) On the journey by sea to Rome, Paul, facing shipwreck and seeming destruction prior to his testimony before the central city of the empire, was comforted by "the angel of God" who stood by him "saying, Fear not, Paul; thou must be brought before Caesar: and, lo, God hath given thee all them that sail with thee." (Acts 27:23-24.)

Paul's experiences teach us much about how God assists and supports his children: After we have made every possible use of prayerful and faithful experience, after we have thought things out in our own minds, finally the Holy Ghost will illuminate the way as we carry the gospel of the Master to every nation.

Chapter Six

Diversity Within Orthodoxy

To this point we have centered primarily upon the crucial events of Paul's life in suggesting certain lessons for us as we take the gospel to every nation. But Paul's teachings, as contained in his epistles, are also directly applicable.

Paul taught that there was a core Christian message that was not to be altered, regardless of the audience to whom it was addressed. This message is preserved for us today primarily but not exclusively in the epistle to the Romans, the first great systematic treatise on Christian theology. While Paul was "all things to all men" as pertaining to outward forms and matters not central to the gospel message, he was also a great prophet of a coming apostasy caused in part by the injection of alien material into Christ's teachings.

Paul taught the Saints in Asia Minor, who were predominantly from pagan backgrounds and were from many lands and nationalities, that they must keep "the unity of the Spirit." There was one body and one Spirit, even as the Saints were called in one hope of their calling: "One Lord, one faith, one baptism, one God and Father of all, who is above all, and through all, and in you all." (Ephesians 4:3-6.)

Paul taught that there was one body and one faith. And yet he spoke of himself as being "all things to all men" in his epistle to another branch of the Church predominantly gentile in membership, the Corinthians.

> And unto the Jews I became as a Jew, that I might gain the Jews; to them that are under the law, as under the law, that I might gain them that are under the law;
> To them that are without law, as without law, (being not without law to God, but under the law to Christ,) that I might gain them that are without law.
> To the weak became I as weak, that I might gain that weak: I am made all things to all men, that I might by all means save some. (1 Corinthians 9:20-22.)

Paul expressed his Jewishness, not only as part of his particular inner being, which it surely was, but also, appropriately, as a means of conveying more central and universal gospel truths to his Hebrew-Christian brethren. He made use of his Roman citizenship at Jerusalem following his arrest, at Caesarea by appealing to Caesar following his trial before Festus, and at Rome itself. He spoke Greek to the Greeks at Athens and Corinth.

Paul demonstrated in his life and in his teachings the proper gospel role of one's own particular culture, politics, and nationality. He himself remained a deeply devout Jew with profound Pharisaical training to the end of his days, insofar as this background was not antithetical to the Christian gospel. He attended the synagogue and the temple; he worshipped at Jerusalem at the Pentecost, even traveling from Greece and Asia Minor to do so. But he did not demand Jewish politics or sociology or belief of a Christian convert not of his background. While the symbolism of Jewry greatly enriched his words to his Hebrew-Christian brethren in the epistle to the Hebrews, quite different symbolism is present in his epistles to the Ephesians, Romans, and Corinthians.

But Paul knew, with a vision perhaps beyond any of his time, the consequences if the gospel core and the Church structure were altered by inclusion of Roman governmental form and pagan philosophy, or if obedience to the Jewish law were established as a requirement of Christian fellowship. To the Saints in Galatia, predominantly gentile, who were intimidated and influenced by the Judaizers, Paul wrote scathing words of rebuke. He marveled that they were "so soon removed" from the grace of Christ "unto another gospel" that was not another but rather a perverted gospel. "But though we, or an angel from heaven, preach any other gospel unto you than that which we have preached unto you, let him be accursed." (Galatians 1:6-8.)

"O foolish Galatians, who hath bewitched you, that ye should not obey the truth, before whose eyes Jesus Christ hath been evidently set forth, crucified among you?" (Galatians 3:1.)

Later in Paul's ministry, between his first and second imprisonments at Rome, he wrote the first of his pastoral epistles to Timothy, his beloved son in the spirit. He warned that the Spirit spoke directly that in the "latter times" some would leave the faith, following "seducing spirits, and doctrines of devils." These apostates would speak "lies in hypocrisy" and would have "their conscience seared with a hot iron; Forbidding to marry, and commanding to abstain from meats, which God hath created to be received with thanksgiving of them which believe and know the truth." (1 Timothy 4:1-3.)

Paul wrote his last testament from his second Roman imprisonment, which he would not survive. Again he wrote to Timothy, who was presiding at Ephesus, with a final warning of apostasy from Christian doctrine and behavior in the perilous "last days":

For men shall be lovers of their own selves, covetous, boasters, proud, blasphemers, disobedient to parents, unthankful, unholy,

Without natural affection, trucebreakers, false accusers, incontinent, fierce, despisers of those that are good,

Traitors, heady, highminded, lovers of pleasures more than lovers of God;

Having a form of godliness, but denying the power thereof: from such turn away.

For of this sort are they which creep into houses, and lead captive silly women laden with sins, led away with divers lusts,

Ever learning, and never able to come to the knowledge of the truth.

Now as Jannes and Jambres withstood Moses, so do these also resist the truth: men of corrupt minds, reprobate concerning the faith. (2 Timothy 3:2-8.)

For the time will come when they will not endure sound doctrine; but after their own lusts shall they heap to themselves teachers, having itching ears;

And they shall turn away their ears from the truth, and shall be turned unto fables. (2 Timothy 4:3-4.)

Paul knew, as surely as anyone could know, that the gospel of his Master was to be maintained in its purity, without debasement or additives.

What, then, was the Christian message that was to be carried to the people of other lands and cultures, free of the politics and sociology of the exporting state?

Most fundamentally, Paul taught that the core of the gospel was the message that Jesus was the Messiah, the Christ. Paul taught with complete faith the divinity of Christ—the spiritual, the miraculous, and the eschatological—as well as the moral role of the Master. That is, he taught that Jesus was the Eternal Son of God who died and atoned for our sins, and who rose from the dead and provided a universal resurrection for all mankind regardless of moral or sacramental act. Further, the atonement provided a means by which we may not only live forever, but also live with the Father and the Son through a redeeming faith that motivates a turning toward God, or repentance, as we "work out [our] own salvation with fear and trembling." (Philemon 2:12.) Finally, the Lord will return to rule over the earth he created. This was the message of universal applicability that transcended divisions of humanity based on nationality or custom: "In whom we have redemption through his blood, even the forgiveness of sins. . . . For by him were all things created, that are in heaven, and that are in earth. . . ." (Colossians 1:14, 16.)

All the epistles of Paul bore special witness to the divinity of the Master: not only did He present the greatest moral teachings the world had known, but through Him and through Him only can mankind obtain eternal life, for "if in this life only we have hope in Christ, we are of all men most miserable." (1 Corinthians 15:19.)

Paul taught the doctrine of atonement with a specificity and depth unmatched even by the writers of the Gospels. Today we unconsciously read into the Gospel accounts of the crucifixion and resurrection a full development of the doctrine of the atonement, which development actually awaited the insight of Paul.

The apostle taught that through the sin of Adam physical death came upon everyone, but that through the atonement of Christ a universal resurrection passed upon all, the just and the unjust. And this was a free gift, extended through the grace of Christ: it was not and could not be earned by moral or ceremonial act:

> Wherefore, as by one man sin entered into the world, and death by sin; and so death passed upon all men, for that all have sinned:
> (For until the law sin was in the world: but sin is not imputed when there is no law.
> Nevertheless death reigned from Adam to Moses. . . .
> For if through the offence of one many be dead, muce more the grace of God, and the gift by grace, which is by one man, Jesus Christ, hath abounded unto many.
> And not as it was by one that sinned, so is the gift: for the judgment was by one to condemnation, but the free gift is of many offences unto justification.
> For if by one man's offence death reigned by one; much more they which receive abundance of grace and of the gift of righteousness shall reign in life by one, Jesus Christ.)
> Therefore as by the offence of one judgment came upon all men to condemnation; even so by the righteousness of one the free gift came upon all men unto justification of life. (Romans 5:12-18.)

He taught with unique power the assurance of the reality of the resurrection:

> Now if Christ be preached that he rose from the dead, how say some among you that there is no resurrection of the dead?
> But if there be no resurrection of the dead, then is Christ not risen:
> And if Christ be not risen, then is our preaching vain, and your faith is also vain.
> If in this life only we have hope in Christ, we are of all men most miserable.
> But now is Christ risen from the dead, and become the firstfruits of them that slept.
> For since by man came death, by man came also the resurrection of the dead.
> For as in Adam all die, even so in Christ shall all be made alive. (1 Corinthians 15:12, 14, 19-22.)

Not only did Paul teach that the atonement of Christ provided a self-executing universal resurrection, but he also taught that the atonement was the integral base of all gospel principles, which were given that man might take on himself more fully the likeness of the Father and the Son. Our eternal life with and like the Father and the Son is based as necessarily upon the atonement as is the

44

universal resurrection. The atonement is "the free gift [which] came upon all men unto justification of life." (Romans 5:18; compare 2 Nephi 2:4.)

> For by grace are ye saved through faith; and that not of yourselves: it is the gift of God:
>
> Not of works, lest any man should boast.
>
> For we are his workmanship, created in Christ Jesus unto good works, which God hath before ordained that we should walk in them. (Ephesians 2:8-10.)

Paul reminds us that the gift of salvation, "the greatest of all the gifts of God" (D&C 14:7), cannot be earned or purchased with earthly goods or human effort. Christ has paid the debt no other mortal could pay; we have no *quid pro quo* to offer him, no means to repay the debt, not even by our works of righteousness or obedience to worshipful ritual.

Yet Paul taught that the Savior had done more than open a door that we could not open ourselves. The Atoning One is also the True Vine in whom we must abide, and He in us, if we are to bring forth fruit. Whether we be wild olive branches, gentiles grafted onto the taproot, or Israelites naturally grown, we progress in the gospel only "by the word of Christ with unshaken faith in him, relying wholly upon the merits of him who is mighty to save." (2 Nephi 31:19.) As we rely upon the grace of Christ, humbling ourselves and exercising faith that he will help us overcome, his grace becomes sufficient for us and his power rests upon us. He transforms our weaknesses into strengths. Our best efforts at moral and spiritual rejuvenation are so entirely dependent upon the precondition of the atonement that we would be unprofitable servants, King Benjamin reminds us, even if we served God with our whole souls all our days. We obtain spiritual "gifts" from God; and "gift" presumes no purchase by others than the Lord. Without such gifts of God, shared with our brothers and sisters in communion and worship together, the body of the Church would not be perfected as we are commanded to become, nor would the Church grow "unto an holy temple in the Lord."

Unlike the resurrection, however, which passes upon all men regardless of moral worth or act, the perfection of the Saints, though as absolutely dependent upon the atonement as is the resurrection, is not self-executing. Our perfection must involve our struggle, even though that struggle is both inspired and blessed by the atonement of the True Vine. It is here that Paul directs us to work out our own salvation with fear and trembling. Paul opposed the fallacy that Bonhoeffer calls "cheap grace " (*The Cost of Discipleship*, p. 41), the notion that salvation in the likeness and the presence of God could be accomplished without total commitment on our own part. With Bonhoeffer, Paul understood the cost of discipleship. Though Jesus said his yoke was light, it was nonetheless a yoke; and Paul, from his conversion, was God's slave, ultimately called (again like Bonhoeffer) to "come and die." (Ibid., p. 7.) Just as Paul understood, with Nephi, that we are saved by grace, "after all we can do" (2 Nephi 25:23), he also warned the wicked of "the day of wrath and revelation of the righteous judgment of God"; God will "render to every man according to his deeds." Those who "by patient continuance in well doing" seek immortality will be rewarded with "eternal life." But those who "do not obey the truth" will be resurrected to an inheritance of "indignation and wrath, tribulation and anguish." (Romans 2:5-9.) Eternal life with and in the image of the Father is a gift, but unlike the unconditional gift of the universal resurrection, it is conditional upon our working out our salvation through the application of saving gospel principles. "For what doth it profit a man if a gift is bestowed upon him, and he receives not the gift? Behold, he rejoices not in that which is given unto him, neither rejoices in him who is the giver of the gift." (D&C 88:33.)

But although eternal life is a gift, one must "qualify" to receive it by observing Christian morality:

What shall we say then? Shall we continue in sin, that grace may abound? God forbid. How shall we, that are dead to sin, live any longer therein?

Know ye not, that so many of us as were baptized into Jesus Christ were baptized into his death?

Therefore we are buried with him by baptism into death: that like as Christ was raised up from the dead by the glory of the Father, even so we also should walk in newness of life.

For if we have been planted together in the likeness of his death, we shall be also in the likeness of his resurrection:

46

Knowing this, that our old man is crucified with him, that the body of sin might be destroyed, that henceforth we should not serve sin. (Romans 6:1-6.)

Paul's epistles not only provide us with the spiritual teachings of Christ's divinity, the atonement and the doctrine of grace, the universal resurrection and the perfection of the Saints, but they are also full of Christian morality, often associated with the teachings of James the Just. Especially to gentile branches from heathen backgrounds, Paul taught austere Christian morality. To the Ephesian Saints and all in Asia Minor he admonished:

This I say . . . that ye henceforth walk not as other Gentiles walk. . . .

Who being past feeling have given themselves over unto lasciviousness, to work all uncleanness with greediness.

But ye have not so learned Christ;

. . . put off . . . the old man, which is corrupt according to the deceitful lusts;

And be renewed in the spirit of your mind;

. . . put on the new man, which after God is created in righteousness and true holiness.

Wherefore put away lying, speak every man truth with his neighbour. . . .

. . . Let not the sun go down upon your wrath:

Neither give place to the devil.

Let him that stole steal no more: but rather let him labour, working with his hands. . . .

. . . grieve not the holy Spirit of God. . . .

Let all bitterness, and wrath, and anger . . . be put away from you, with all malice:

And be ye kind to one another, tenderhearted, forgiving one another, even as God for Christ's sake hath forgiven you. (Ephesians 4:17-32.)

And the Saints at Corinth:

Know ye not that ye are the temple of God, and that the Spirit of God dwelleth in you?

If any man defile the temple of God, him shall God destroy; for the temple of God is holy, which temple ye are. (1 Corinthians 3:16-17.)

Paul constantly warned the gentile converts of pagan background to avoid the shameful immorality of the heathen. The gentile pagan converts had been "sometimes darkness" but were now "children of light" who must not again be "partakers with

47

them" of immoral practices. They were to have "no fellowship with the unfruitful works of darkness"; the Christian Saint was to "walk circumspectly" because "the days are evil" (Ephesians 5:7-16):

> Wherefore take unto you the whole armour of God, that ye may be able to withstand in the evil day, and having done all, to stand.
> Stand therefore, having your loins girt about with truth, and having on the breastplate of righteousness;
> And your feet shod with the preparation of the gospel of peace;
> Above all, taking the shield of faith, wherewith ye shall be able to quench all the fiery darts of the wicked.
> And take the helmet of salvation, and the sword of the Spirit, which is the word of God. (Ephesians 6:13-17.)

Finally, Paul taught of a literal second advent of the Master, when he would rule over the earth that he created: "For the Lord himself shall descend from heaven with a shout, with the voice of the archangel, and with the trump of God." (1 Thessalonians 4:16.)

Paul, then, taught a universal Christian gospel to Greeks and Romans, gentiles and Jews. This gospel was centered upon the spiritual, eschatological, and moral teachings of Christ: Jesus Christ is literally the Son of God; he accomplished an atonement and by that means overcame physical death for all by grace with universal resurrection of the body; the atonement provides as well the opportunity by which we "work out our own salvation," after which we are saved by the grace of God.

In addition to that important foundation teaching, Paul taught that the Church had a particular role in the propagation and administration of Christ's gospel. Christ taught that the moral injunctions of his Sermon on the Mount were given that Christian Saints could "be . . . perfect, even as your Father which is in heaven is perfect." (Matthew 5:48.) For Paul, the role of the Church was to provide a community within which such teachings could be taught and practiced, and saving ordinances authoritatively performed. Thus our divine destiny—the ultimate fulfillment of our creation in the image of God—could be accomplished:

> And he gave some, apostles; and some, prophets; and some, evangelists; and some, pastors and teachers;

For the perfecting of the saints, for the work of the ministry, for the edifying of the body of Christ:

Till we all come in the unity of the faith, and of the knowledge of the Son of God, unto a perfect man, unto the measure of the stature of the fulness of Christ. (Ephesians 4:11-13.)

Coupled with the spiritual, eschatological, and moral teachings of Christ, joined with the role of the Church, Paul taught as part of the universal core of Christian teachings certain "first principles" by which the Christian Saint sought perfection.

First, Christian faith was that bedrock principle which replaced the outward forms of the Mosaic law. Christian faith was knowledge set on fire. Pauline faith virtually subsumed all other principles because it was the motivating force leading to them; with faith present, all else would naturally follow:

Now we know that what things soever the law saith, it saith to them who are under the law: that every mouth may be stopped, and all the world may become guilty before God.

Therefore by the deeds of the law there shall no flesh be justified in his sight: for by the law is the knowledge of sin.

But now the righteousness of God without the law is manifested, being witnessed by the law and the prophets;

Even the righteousness of God which is by faith of Jesus Christ unto all and upon all them that believe: for there is no difference:

For all have sinned, and come short of the glory of God;

Being justified freely by his grace through the redemption that is in Christ Jesus:

Whom God hath set forth to be a propitiation through faith in his blood, to declare his righteousness for the remission of sins that are past, through the forebearance of God. . . .

Where is boasting then? It is excluded. By what law? of works? Nay: but by the law of faith.

Therefore we conclude that a man is justified by faith without the deeds of the law.

Is he the God of the Jews only? is he not also of the Gentiles? Yes, of the Gentiles also:

Seeing it is one God, which shall justify the circumcision by faith, and uncircumcision through faith. (Romans 3:19-30.)

Paul taught the same first principle of faith not only to the churches at Rome, which must have been composed largely of gentile members of pagan background, but also to his Hebrew-Christian brethren at Jerusalem and elsewhere throughout the Church. He explained in the epistle to the Hebrews that it was by faith that Abel "offered unto God a more excellent sacrifice"; it was by faith that "Enoch was translated that he should not see death"; by faith "Noah . . . prepared an ark to the saving of his house"; by faith Abraham received "an inheritance" and "looked for a city which hath foundations, whose builder and maker is God"; through faith "Sara . . . received strength to conceive"; by faith Moses "forsook Egypt," "kept the passover," and "passed through the Red sea"; by faith "the walls of Jericho fell down." (Hebrews 11.)

Paul taught both gentiles and Jews the first principle of faith. Though he used examples of Israelite history to teach his Hebrew brethren, and removed such examples for the churches at Rome, the message was the same. And with the first principle Paul taught the second: faith and grace through Christ's atonement were to be accompanied by repentance and baptism.

Repentance, a turning to God, was a natural, almost inevitable consequence of Christian faith and became a continuing process: increasing Godlike sensitivity led to continuing repentance and refinement; then to discipleship and conversion; always to the increasing likeness of the Father and the Son. Paul observed this process among the Corinthian Saints. In his first epistle to the Corinthians, he had chastised them sharply for the pagan sinfulness and immorality still among them. Between the time of the arrival of the first epistle, which the Corinthian Saints received as severe rebuke, and Paul's writing of Second Corinthians, Titus visited them on behalf of Paul. Titus found that the Corinthians had sorrowed to the accomplishment of repentance and so reported to Paul. The apostle then wrote again to the Saints at Corinth:

> For though I made you sorry with a letter, I do not repent . . . for I perceive that the same epistle hath made you sorry, though it were but for a season.
>
> Now I rejoice, not that ye were made sorry, but that ye sorrowed to repentance: for ye were made sorry after a godly manner. . . .
>
> For godly sorrow worketh repentance to salvation not to be repented of: but the sorrow of the world worketh death. (2 Corinthians 7:8-10.)

Baptism of water allowed a forgiveness of sins and marked the entrance of the Christian Saint into the kingdom of God. Baptism of the Spirit followed. The powerful and deep symbolism of the baptismal ordinance was captured by Paul in words to the Saints at Rome:

> Know ye not, that so many of us as were baptized into Jesus Christ were baptized into his death?
>
> Therefore we are buried with him by baptism into death: that like as Christ was raised up from the dead by the glory of the Father, even so we also should walk in newness of life.
>
> For if we have been planted together in the likeness of his death, we shall be also in the likeness of his resurrection:
>
> Knowing this, that our old man is crucified with him, that the body of sin might be destroyed, that henceforth we should not serve sin. (Romans 6:3-6.)

Paul, even after receiving a direct revelation from the Master, was nevertheless told to repent from the whole course of his previous life, be baptized at Ananias's hands, and receive the Holy Ghost. He stands as an example that none are exempt from those requirements.

This then was the core of the Christian gospel: Jesus was the Christ, the Messiah who had come to atone for the sins of all humanity, provide for a universal resurrection, present his example and his teachings for the perfection of the Saints, and endow a church with authority to teach the gospel and administer saving ordinances, including baptism and the bestowal of the Holy Spirit upon those who had faith in the Lord and repented of sinful lives. Finally, a Messianic second advent was promised in which the Master would rule over the earth he had created.

Chapter Seven

No More Strangers and Foreigners

In addition to the identification of a core Christian gospel that could be carried to all people, and the elaboration of "first principles" of that gospel, Paul through his epistles made other seminal contributions to the interpretation and propagation of the faith of his Master.

Paul's most unusual contribution as "a chosen vessel" to bear Christ's name "before the Gentiles, and kings, and the children of Israel" (Acts 9:15) was in his early and complete perception of the universality of the Christian message; it was not for the Jew only, nor was it limited to the Roman, the Greek, to the master or the slave. This insight, demonstrated in his life as we have discussed, was eloquently taught in his letters. This unique contribution of Paul's finds perhaps its most beautiful and most powerful expression in the second and third chapters of the epistle to the Ephesians. He speaks of the earlier division of mankind into gentiles and Jews, the former being "aliens from the commonwealth of Israel," "strangers from the covenants of promise, having no hope," being unable by law to progress beyond the middle wall of the temple.

But now in Christ Jesus ye who sometimes were far off are made nigh by the blood of Christ.

For he is our peace, who hath made both one, and hath broken down the middle wall of partition between us. . . .

Now therefore ye are no more strangers and foreigners, but fellowcitizens with the saints, and of the household of God;

And are built upon the foundation of the apostles and prophets, Jesus Christ himself being the chief corner stone;

In whom all the building fitly framed together groweth unto an holy temple in the Lord. (Ephesians 2:12-22. See also Romans 3.)

This vision of the universality of the gospel made possible its triumph over the circumscriptions of nationality, race, and sect, so that Christianity would expand to the limits of the Roman Empire and ultimately burst even those bonds. Outward things, peculiarities of the ceremonial law, of nationality, or of race, were not to be prerequisite either to baptism or to full Christian fellowship: "Him who is weak in his faith receive into your fellowship, imposing no determination of doubtful questions." (Romans 14:1, Conybeare translation. See Romans 14 and 1 Corinthians 8.)

Related to his concept of the universality of the gospel, Paul taught that salvation could not come through the legalism of ceremonial law but rather through the atonement of Jesus Christ. A "new Israel" had been created, not by the ceremonial law whose symbolism looked forward to the coming of the Messiah, but by faith in the Messiah who had come. The law was a schoolmaster to prepare a people for the coming of the Messiah. The Christian Saint must move beyond legalism and outward forms to the inward life of moral rectitude and abiding faith. If the law were to become an end in itself rather than a teaching step in the ladder toward faith in Christ and in his atonement, then the law would become an impediment to truth. The law by itself could not save. Only the atonement of Christ could accomplish salvation through the extension of his grace. And perfection came by the possession of faith sufficient to abide his teachings.

We who are Jews by nature, and not sinners of the Gentiles,

Knowing that a man is not justified by the works of the law, but by the faith of Jesus Christ, even we have believed in Jesus Christ, that we might be justified by the faith of Christ, and not by the works of the law: for by the works of the law shall no flesh be justified. . . .

I do not frustrate the grace of God: for if righteousness come by the law, then Christ is dead in vain.

O foolish Galatians, who hath bewitched you, that ye should not obey the truth, before whose eyes Jesus Christ hath been evidently set forth crucified among you?

This only would I learn of you, Received ye the Spirit by the works of the law, or by the hearing of faith?

Are ye so foolish? having begun in the Spirit, are ye now made perfect by the flesh?

Have ye suffered so many things in vain? if it be yet in vain.

He therefore that ministereth to you the Spirit, and worketh miracles among you, doeth he it by the works of the law, or by the hearing of faith?

Even as Abraham believed God, and it was accounted to him for righteousness.

Know ye therefore that they which are of faith, the same are the children of Abraham.

And the scripture, foreseeing that God would justify the heathen through faith, preached before the gospel unto Abraham, saying, In thee shall all nations be blessed.

So then they which be of faith are blessed with faithful Abraham. . . .

But before faith came, we were kept under the law, shut up unto the faith which should afterwards be revealed.

Wherefore the law was our schoolmaster to bring us unto Christ, that we might be justified by faith.

But after that faith is come, we are no longer under a schoolmaster.

For ye are all the children of God by faith in Christ Jesus. . . .

And if ye be Christ's, then are ye Abraham's seed, and heirs according to the promise. (Galatians 2:15-16, 21; 3:1-9, 23-26, 29.)

This teaching, which led to continual harassment by the Judaizers and eventually to Paul's death, also ensured the success of the early Church and the place of Paul as the greatest missionary the Christian faith has ever known.

Paul's spirit of universality and his objection to sterile legalism were founded upon his understanding that love, not legalism, was at the heart of the Christian gospel. This concept of love recognized the inextricable linkage between love of God as our Father and love of our fellowmen as our brothers and sisters, in all basic aspects indistinguishable from ourselves, whom we are also to love. For Paul, the concept of *neighbor*, whom we were commanded to love, extended beyond those artificial boundaries of race or nationality to encompass all of God's children.

He who loves his neighbour has fulfilled the law.

For the law which says, 'Thou shalt not commit adultery; Thou shalt do no murder; Thou shalt not steal; Thou shalt not bear false witness; Thou shalt not covet' (and whatsoever other commandment there be,) is all contained in this one saying, 'Thou shalt love thy neighbour as thyself.'

Love works no ill to his neighbour; therefore Love is the fulfilment of the law. (Romans 13:8-10, Conybeare translation.)

Paul's priceless sermon on Christian love, translated *charity* by the King James scholars, has become one of the treasures of all scripture.

I may speak in tongues of men or of angels, but if I am without love, I am a sounding gong or a clanging cymbal. I may have the gift of prophecy, and know every hidden truth; I may have faith strong enough to move mountains; but if I have no love, I am nothing. I may dole out all I possess, or even give my body to be burnt, but if I have no love, I am none the better.

Love is patient; love is kind and envies no one. Love is never boastful, nor conceited, nor rude; never selfish, not quick to take offence. Love keeps no score of wrongs; does not gloat over other men's sins, but delights in the truth. There is nothing love cannot face; there is no limit to its faith, its hope, and its endurance.

Love will never come to an end. Are there prophets? their work will be over. Are there tongues of ecstasy? they will cease. Is there knowledge? it will vanish away; for our knowledge and our prophecy alike are partial, and the partial vanishes when wholeness comes. When I was a child, my speech, my outlook, and my thoughts were all childish. When I grew up, I had finished with childish things. Now we see only puzzling reflections in a mirror, but then we shall see face to face. My knowledge now is partial; then it will be whole, like God's knowledge of me. In a word, there are three things that last for ever: faith, hope, and love; but the greatest of them all is love. (1 Corinthians 13, New English Bible.)

The gospel principles Paul preached to people of other cultures were more readily acceptable to them because they were universal principles, separated from the politics and the social customs of any one culture. In perceiving earlier than his brethren the necessity of such a separation if the gospel was to be preached to every nation, Paul demonstrated those characteristics of soul for which the Lord selected him as "a light of the Gentiles" for "salvation unto the ends of the earth." (Acts 13:46-47.)

But Paul's personal life of worship demonstrated also the analogue to the rule of universality: that every culture upon reception of the gospel is able to apply its principles within the matrix of its own political institutions and social customs, insofar as they are compatible with the gospel. In this manner the symbols native to the local community can be used with all the strength generated by their congruence and coherence with the community of which they are a natural part.

Paul, Peter and the others of the Twelve Apostles, and indeed the entire Jewish-Christian community of the first century, demonstrated this by maintaining with integrity their fidelity to Jewish practice and worship, even while they lived the Christian gospel. But as great missionaries, with Christian love for others superseding the natural egotistical tendency to identify one's own culture with eternal principles, James, Peter, Paul, and the other Jewish-Christian leaders determined to separate the gospel from their own sociology before they took it to other cultures. Thus they laid upon the people of other cultures no greater burden than the necessary things. To do otherwise, to demand the acceptance of alien social customs as if they were part of gospel principles, would limit the receiving culture to the use of alien symbols, which would be impotent and unlikely to take natural root. The power of word symbols depends upon the familiarity of the community with the example, the metaphor, the simile. And such partially nonverbal symbols as are accomplished through music and architecture must be naturally coherent with the community if the symbols are to be able to speak more deeply to our souls, at times beneath our very consciousness, to deepen our worship, motivate our repentance, and assure us of God's love.

The apostles made this distinction between gospel doctrine and social custom for the sake of the gentiles they were seeking to convert. But it is more difficult to make that distinction within one's own culture, for the purpose of one's own worship. Such choice is made more difficult, among other reasons, because in this case both customs and doctrine are natural to one's own society, and both are desired. But when a missionary deals with another culture, his social customs are not necessarily desired by his new converts to the doctrine. Consequently, one who would attempt such a distinguishment for the well-being of his own people, for their own worship, could well be resented or considered disloyal or traitorous. Herein Paul was a "chosen vessel," not only "before the Gentiles, and kings," but to his own "children of Israel" as well. (Acts 9:15.)

Paul possessed a tenderness toward people of narrower vision and spirit that allowed him to present his infinitely broader views with compassion and understanding. This characteristic, as much as any other, must account for his success as a missionary among people of other lands. In speaking to the gentile Christians about their freedom from living the Jewish ceremonial law, he noted:

> But meat commendeth us not to God: for neither, if we eat, are we the better; neither, if we eat not, are we the worse.
>
> But take heed lest by any means this liberty of yours become a stumblingblock to them that are weak.
>
> For if any man see thee which hast knowledge sit at meat in the idol's temple, shall not the conscience of him which is weak be emboldened to eat those things which are offered to idols;
>
> And through thy knowledge shall the weak brother perish, for whom Christ died? But when ye sin so against the brethren, and wound their weak conscience, ye sin against Christ. (1 Corinthians 8:8-12.)

No more profound example of this capacity lovingly to convey the more universal insight can be found than Paul's epistle to the Hebrews,[1] written to Hebrew Christians suffering acutely after

---

[1] The epistle to the Hebrews poses special problems in terms of authorship. Alone among the epistles ascribed to Paul, it contains no identification of authorship or church to which it was directed. In assuming Pauline authorship I have not overlooked the arguments made by scholars and churchmen, from the second coming to the present time, which conclude differently. Conybeare (p. 784) notes correctly that "there is no portion of the New Testament whose authorship is so disputed, nor any of which the inspiration is more indisputable."

The eastern churches have from the first century considered Paul to be the author of Hebrews; the western church disputed Pauline authorship until the fourth century. Tertullian and the churches of North Africa ascribed the epistle to Barnabas. (Conybeare, p. 788; Hastings' *Dictionary of the Bible*, p. 370.) Tertullian, in fact, reported that the copies of the epistle to the Hebrews extant in his day were entitled "The epistle of Barnabas to the Hebrews." (Conybeare, p. 788; Smith's *Bible Dictionary*, p. 773.) The oldest manuscripts now in existence say simply "To the Hebrews." (Dummelow, p. 1012.) Jerome reported that some in the early church considered the thoughts and theology to be Paul's but that Luke or Clement of Rome organized and transcribed the epistle. (Conybeare, p. 788; Smith, p. 733; Hastings, p. 370.)

Adolphe von Harnack believed the author of the epistle to the Hebrews to have been Priscilla, who did not sign it because of the bias against women in such a role. (Dummelow, p. 1012.) The superb new translation of the Bible for Roman Catholic worship, the Jerusalem Bible, credits Apollos as the most likely author of Hebrews (p. 265), as does Farrar (p. 6, n. 1).

Eusebius, the first great church historian, said that the epistle is generally the work of Paul; he refrained from signing the epistle because of the hostility felt toward him by many Hebrew Christians. (*Euseb. Eccl. Hist.* vi 14.) Chrysostom agreed with this. (Smith, p. 773.) Clement of Rome considered Paul

having been refused the right to participate in the temple service—unless they would deny their Christian beliefs. Until the death of James the Just, evidently Jame's awesome integrity and reputation among non-Christian Jews alike had been sufficient to assure the Christian Jew the right to participate in the Jewish temple service and in his own Christian communion together. But with the assassination of James, a drive was begun to purify Jewish worship of Christian participation. For the first time for many Jewish Christians, they had to choose between their Jewishness and their Christianity. And choosing Christianity would leave them separated from the temple, which was at once their preeminent religious and their national symbol.

In the context of this crisis for Jewish Christianity, we see once again the manner in which Paul was able to distinguish between the gospel core—the mission of Jesus as the Christ—and Hebrew sociology, including the symbolism of the Jewish faith. During Paul's earlier ministry, he, with the other Church leaders, had been required to distinguish between custom and doctrine for the benefit of gentile Christianity. Now he had to accomplish a similar distinguishment for Hebrew Christians who were forced for the first time to discriminate between essential gospel principles and certain parts of the Jewish faith, such as temple worship. Jewish temple worship was not necessarily antithetical to Christianity, and therefore it had been participated in by Jewish Christians; but for the Christian it was not essential to salvation; it was part of a sociological matrix rather than the gospel's core.

Neither Paul nor any of the Twelve at Jerusalem had ever attempted to discourage Jewish Christians from participating in

---

to be the author of an original epistle to the Hebrew written in Hebrew, which was translated into Greek by Luke (Smith, p. 773), thus accounting for a similarity of style between Acts and Uebrews.

The assignment of the epistle to the Hebrews from tenth place in the Greek canon to fourteenth at the end of Paul's epistles, and before the other apostles' epistles, indicated a rather universal acceptance by the Greek and Latin churches by the end of the fourth century that Hebrews is canonical and is Pauline in theology and thought, but not in the same full and undisputed sense of total authorship as were the other Pauline epistles. (Smith, p. 774.)

The weight of evidence and authority would certainly indicate that the theology is Paul's; the canonicity of Hebrews is unquestioned; for the purposes of this volume, therefore, it is inconsequential whether Luke influenced its style in translation to Clement through organization. All possible "authors" or "influences" of Hebrews—Apollos, Priscilla, Clement, Barnabas, and Luke—bore the overwhelming influence of the great Apostle to the Gentiles. For me, the epistle is correctly titled: The Epistle of Paul to the Hebrews.

Jewish religious activity, including the services of the synagogue and the temple. On the contrary, Paul and Peter and the Twelve participated fully in Jewish ceremony, along with Jewish Christians generally, throughout the first century of the Christian era.

But now that which was not central to salvation had to be distinguished from that which was. And the distinguishment had to be made not for those who hoped to be able to avoid the burden of Jewish law, but on behalf of those who, like Paul himself, had grown up immersed in Jewish culture, who loved with every fiber of their being the intense ceremony of the temple service; who saw Jewish law as the epitome of their nationality, their society, and their religion.

The apostle Paul writes to his Hebrew-Christian brethren as high priest to high priests, pleading with them not to forsake the inner Christian morality and the promise of eternal life for the outward ceremonialism of the law, even the law of the sacred temple ceremony.

The tender sensitivity with which this is done marks Paul as a man among men. He explains with loving kindness that Judaic ceremonialism was only a type, an earthly Levitical precursor or forerunner of Christianity, which had a new high priest, Jesus, after the order of Melchizedek:

Wherefore, holy brethren, partakers of the heavenly calling, consider the Apostle and High Priest of our profession, Christ Jesus;

Who was . . . faithful in all his house.

For this man was counted worthy of more glory than Moses, inasmuch as he who hath builded the house hath more honour than the house.

For every house is builded by some man; but he that built all things is God.

And Moses verily was faithful in all his house, as a servant, for a testimony of those things which were to be spoken after;

But Christ as a son over his own house; whose house are we, if we hold fast the confidence and the rejoicing of the hope firm unto the end. (Hebrews 3:1-6.)

If therefore perfection were by the Levitical priesthood, (for under it the people received the law,) what further need was there that another priest should rise after the order of Melchisedec, and not be called after the order of Aaron? (Hebrews 7:11.)

Paul taught his Hebrew brethren that the legalism of constant sin offerings was no longer necessary because of the infinite atonement of Jesus Christ, for which the former was simply a symbolic forerunner. It would be awful irony to remain tied to the ceremonial form that originally was designed to prepare a people for the reality of an Atoning One, when in fact such a One had come. Further, bad psychology was employed when one insisted upon a recurring reminder of sin even though the atonement, coupled with repentance, meant that sin was to be remembered no more. The gospel of Jesus Christ is to produce inner morality, and outward ceremony cannot suffice for such inward virtue:

For the law having a shadow of good things to come, and not the very image of the things, can never with those sacrifices which they offered year by year continually make the comers thereunto perfect.

For then would they not have ceased to be offered? because that the worshippers once purged should have had no more conscience of sins.

But in those sacrifices there is a remembrance again made of sins every year.

For it is not possible that the blood of bulls and of goats should take away sins. . . .

By the which will we are sanctified through the offering of the body of Jesus Christ once for all.

And every priest standeth daily ministering and offering oftentimes the same sacrifices, which can never take away sins:

But this man, after he had offered one sacrifice for sins for ever, sat down on the right hand of God; . . .

This is the covenant that I will make with them after those days, saith the Lord, I will put my laws into their hearts, and in their minds will I write them;

And their sins and iniquities will I remember no more.

Now where remission of these is, there is no more offering for sin.

Having therefore, brethren, boldness to enter into the holiest by the blood of Jesus,

By a new and living way, which he hath consecrated for us, through the veil, that is to say, his flesh;

And having an high priest over the house of God;

Let us draw near with a true heart in full assurance of faith, having our hearts sprinkled from an evil conscience, and our bodies washed with pure water. (Hebrews 10:1-4, 10-12, 16-22.)

Paul taught his Hebrew-Christian brethren that Christianity demanded no rejection of their Jewishness, but rather a recognition of its glorious fulfillment in the Christ.

If therefore perfection were by the Levitical priesthood, (for under it the people received the law,) what further need was there that another priest should rise after the order of Melchisedec, and not be called after the order of Aaron? . . .

For it is evident that our Lord sprang out of Juda; of which tribe Moses spake nothing concerning priesthood. (Hebrews 7:11, 14.)

Now of the things which we have spoken this is the sum: We have such a high priest, who is set on the right hand of the throne of the Majesty in the heavens;

A minister of the sanctuary, and of the true tabernacle, which the Lord pitched, and not man. (Hebrews 8:1-2.)

Then verily the first covenant had also ordinances of divine service, and a worldly sanctuary. . . .

But Christ being come an high priest of good things to come, by a greater and more perfect tabernacle, not made with hands, that is to say, not of this building;

Neither by the blood of goats and calves, but by his own blood he entered in once into the holy place, having obtained eternal redemption for us.

For if the blood of bulls and of goats, and the ashes of an heifer sprinkling the unclean, sanctifieth to the purifying of the flesh:

How much more shall the blood of Christ, who through the eternal Spirit offered himself without spot to God, purge your conscience from dead works to serve the living God?

And for this cause he is the mediator of the new testament, that by means of death, for the redemption of the transgressions that were under the first testament, they which are called might receive the promise of eternal inheritance. (Hebrews 9:1, 11-15.)

Paul taught his Christian-Hebrew brethren, who soon would have to face the destruction of the holy city Jerusalem and the further disintegration of their nationhood, that the gospel promised something better, a heavenly city, the City of God. Speaking of the faith of Abel, Enoch, Noah, Abraham, and Moses, each of whom gave up his earthly community as a supreme act of faith, Paul noted:

For they that say such things declare plainly that they seek a country.

And truly, if they had been mindful of that country from whence they came out, they might have had opportunity to have returned.

But now they desire a better country, that is, an heavenly: wherefore God is not ashamed to be called their God: for he hath prepared for them a city. (Hebrews 11:14-16.)

Though he could love his own country and the traditions of his society that did not conflict with the gospel of the Master, ultimate fidelity for the Christian Saint was to no earthly place or ruler. Final allegiance must be to the Father and the Son, or the first commandment would be violated. And the Christian citizen of the kingdom of God was, at best, a sojourner upon the land; his ultimate allegiance was to no earthly country, but to Zion. Only there could Israel "obey [God's] voice indeed, and keep [his] covenant" and become to Jehovah "a kingdom of priests." (Exodus 19:5-6.) For the Christian longed for the perfect community, to be inhabited by the pure in heart.

"But ye are come unto Mount Sion, and unto the city of the living God, the heavenly Jerusalem, and to an innumerable company of angels, To the general assembly and church of the firstborn, which are written in heaven, and to God the Judge of all, and to the spirits of just men made perfect." (Hebrews 12:22-23.)

"For here have we no continuing city, but we seek one to come." (Hebrews 13:14.)

William Smith has observed that the epistle to the Hebrews "is a pattern to every Christian teacher of the method in which larger views should be imparted, gently, reverently, and seasonally, to feeble spirits prone to cling to ancient forms, and to rest in accustomed feelings." (*Dictionary of the Bible* 2:1029.)

Paul, by his choice of every metaphor, simile, and parable, demonstrated his belief in the absolute necessity of the integration of Christian worship, with a Church membership that at once recognized and appreciated each other's distinct individuality, but at the same time rejected a caste system based upon any such distinctions. This essential point was forcefully made by Paul in his public rebuke of Peter when the latter separated himself from eating with gentile Christians at Antioch. (Galatians 2:11-16.) Jew and gentile, Roman and Greek were part of the interdependent "body of Christ," in which the ear cannot say, "Because I am not the eye, I am not of the body." (1 Corinthians 12:12-20.) Again, the Church membership are building blocks "in whom all the building fitly framed together groweth unto an holy temple in the Lord." (Ephesians 2:19-21.) And again, Israel and the gentile nations are likened to natural and wild olive branches which, in abrasive yet positive dialectic, should stimulate each other to good works: the Hebrew to learn Christian truth of the freedom from dead works of the law, while both learn Christian love together. (Romans 11:16-18.) The Hebrew Christian is commanded not to judge his gentile brother, not the gentile Christian despise his Hebrew-Christian brother: "Let not him that eateth despise him that eateth not; and let not him which eateth not judge him that eateth: for God hath received him." (Romans 14:3.)

Diversities of spiritual gifts are given, one gift to one member, another to another, that together members may bless themselves and each other. To one may be given great faith, to another knowledge. The gift of healing may be given to another, and spiritual interpretation to someone else. But all must work together so that each member may enrich and bless his brother and, indirectly, himself, through losing and therefore finding his life in service to others.

While Paul's sermon on spiritual gifts has an obvious reference to individuals as well, different nations and peoples can also contribute uniquely to each other in Christian fellowship. Every political group and nation, each a startlingly, refreshingly different community—from Arab lands to Asia, Africa, and Latin America—can add to the richness and the texture of our Christian community. Every race and every people truly become a building block in which each, fitly framed together, grows unto a holy temple in the Lord. Every kindred and nation become part of the interdependent body of Christ in fellowship and in worship:

> For as the body is one, and hath many members, and all the members of that one body, being many, are one body: so also is Christ.
> For by one Spirit are we all baptized into one body, whether we be Jews or Gentiles, whether we be bond or free; and have been all made to drink into one Spirit.
> For the body is not one member, but many.
> If the foot shall say, Because I am not the hand, I am not of the body; is it therefore not of the body?
> And if the ear shall say, Because I am not the eye, I am not of the body; is it therefore not of the body?
> If the whole body were an eye, where were the hearing? If the whole were hearing, where were the smelling?

But now hath God set the members every one of them in the body, as it hath pleased him.

And if they were all one member, where were the body?

But now are they many members, yet but one body. (1 Corinthians 12:12-20.)

The apostle Paul has provided the preeminent example by which we transcend differences of nationality, forms of government, and social customs, by preaching a universal gospel that is not limited by the peculiar characteristics of a particular time or place. No greater burden than these necessary things of salvation through Christ's gospel are to be demanded of the investigator from another land or culture. Each people—within the parameter of consistency with the gospel's core—may live the gospel of the Master and at the same time maintain fidelity to the politics and the social customs of their land.

In this manner may we abide the admonition of the Apostle to the Gentiles that we "receive . . . one another, as Christ also received us to the glory of God." (Romans 15:7.) With Paul, we say to our brothers and sisters of every land: "Now therefore ye are no more strangers and foreigners, but fellowcitizens with the saints, and of the household of God." (Ephesians 2:19.)

Selected Bibliography

Ackroyd, P.R., and Evans, C.F., eds. *The Cambridge History of the Bible.* 3 vols. London: Cambridge University Press, 1970.

Aharoni, Yohanon, and Avi-Yonah, Michael. *The Macmillan Bible Atlas.* 2d ed., rev. New York: Macmillan Publishing Co., Inc., 1977.

Attiya, Aziz S. *The Copts and Christian Civilization.* Salt Lake City: University of Utah Press, 1979.

_____. *History of Eastern Christianity.* Notre Dame, Ind.: University of Notre Dame Press, 1968.

Barker, James L. *Apostasy from the Divine Church.* Salt Lake City: Deseret Book Co., 1960.

_____. *The Protestors of Christendom.* Independence, Mo.: Zion's Printing & Publishing Company, 1946.

_____. *The Restoration of the Divine Church.* Salt Lake City: Kate Montgomery Barker, 1962.

Ben-Sason, H.H., ed. *A History of the Jewish People.* Cambridge, Mass.: Harvard University Press, 1976.

Bonhoeffer, Dietrich. *The Cost of Discipleship.* New York: Macmillan Publishing Co., Inc., 1974.

Clark, J. Reuben, Jr. *On the Way to Immortality and Eternal Life.* Salt Lake City: Deseret Book Co., 1949.

Conybeare, W.J., and Howson, J.S. *The Life and Epistles of St. Paul.* London: Longmans, Green & Co., 1887.

Davidson, F., et al., eds. *The New Bible Commentary.* London: Inter-Varsity Fellowship, 1954.

Duchesne, Monsignor Louis. *Early History of the Christian Church: From Its Foundations to the End of the Fifth Century.* 3 vols. London: John Murray, 1933.

Dummelow, J.R. *The One Volume Bible Commentary.* London: Macmillan & Co., 1909.

Etheridge, J.W., trans. *The Apostolic Acts and Epistles, Translated from the Syriac.* London: Longman, Brown, Green & Longmans, 1849.

Farrar, Frederick W. *Darkness and Dawn: Scenes in the Days of Nero.* London: Longmans, Green & Co., 1924.

_____. *The Early Days of Christianity.* London: Cassell, Peter, Galpin & Co., 1882.

_____. *Life and Work of St. Paul.* London: Cassell & Co., n.d.

_____. *Lives of the Fathers.* 2 vols. Edinburgh: Adam & Chas. Black, 1889.

_____. *The Messages of the Books.* London: Macmillan & Co., 1892.

Goodspeed, Edgar. *The Story of the Bible.* Chicago: University of Chicago Press, 1936.

Grant, Michael. *A History of Rome.* New York: Charles Scribner & Sons, 1978.

Hastings, James, ed. *Dictionary of the Bible.* Rev. ed., F. Grant & H.H. Rowley. New York: Charles Scribner & Sons, 1963.

Holy Bible, King James Version. Cambridge, England: Cambridge University Press.

Holy Bible, Revised Edition. London: Oxford University Press, 1898.

Holy Bible, Revised Standard Version. Edinburgh: Thomas Nelson & Sons, Ltd., 1956.

Holy Bible, Translated from the Latin Vulgate. London: Burns, Oates & Washbourne, Ltd., 1914.

Jerusalem Bible. Alexander Jones, ed. Garden City, N.Y.: Doubleday, 1966.

Johnson, Paul. *A History of Christianity*. New York: Atheneum Press, 1976.

Kierkegaard, Soren. *Fear and Trembling*. Copenhagen, 1843.

Knox, Ronald, and Cox, Ronald. *It Is Paul Who Writes*. New York: Theed and Ward, 1944.

Lake, Kirsopp. *The Apostolic Fathers*. 2 vols. London: William Herremann, 1914.

Lightfoot, J.B. *St. Paul's Epistle to the Galatians*. London: Macmillan & Co., 1896.

Moffatt, James. *An Introduction to the Literature of the New Testament*. Edinburgh: T. & T. Clark, 1912.

_____. *The New Testament: A New Translation*. London: Hodder & Staughton, 1913.

Neander, Augustus. *Lectures on the History of Christian Dogmas*. 2 vols. London: Bell & Doldy, 1866.

Neill, Stephen. *A History of Christian Missions*. Baltimore: Penguin Books, 1964.

New American Bible. Camden, N.J.: Thomas Nelson, Inc., 1971.

New English Bible. London: Oxford University Press, 1961.

Nibley, Hugh. *The Timely and the Timeless*. Salt Lake City: Publishers Press, 1978.

Plummer, Alfred. *The Church of the Early Fathers*. London: Longmans, Green & Co., 1892.

Ramsay, William. *Pictures of the Apostolic Church*. London: Hodder & Staughton, 1910.

Roberts, Alexander, and Donaldson, James, eds. *Ante-Nicene Christian Library*. 23 vols. Edinburgh: T. & T. Clark, 1920.

Salmon, George. *An Historical Introduction to the Study of the Books of the New Testament*. 9th ed. London: John Murray, 1904.

Smith, David. *The Life and Letters of St. Paul*. London: Hodder and Staughton, Ltd., 1921.

Smith, Joseph. *History of the Church*. 7 vols. Salt Lake City: Deseret Book Company, 1975.

Smith, Joseph F. *Gospel Doctrine*. Salt Lake City: Deseret Book Company, 1963.

Smith, Philip. *The History of the Christian Church*. 2 vols. London: John Murray, 1902.

Smith, William. *A Dictionary of the Bible*. 3 vols. London: John Murray, 1863.

Smyth, J. Paterson. *The Ancient Documents and the Modern Bible*. London: Sampson, Low, Marston & Co.

Sperry, Sidney B. *Paul's Life and Letters*. Salt Lake City: Bookcraft, 1955.

Tillich, Paul. *A History of Christian Thought*. New York: Simon & Schuster, 1968.

Von Harnack, Adolf. *The Acts of the Apostles*. New York: Williams & Norgate, 1909.

_____. *The Constitution and Law of the Church in the First Two Centuries*. New York: G.P. Putnam & Sons, 1910.

_____. *History of Dogma*. Edwin Know Mitchell, trans. London: Hodder & Staughton, 1893.

_____. *The Origin of the New Testament*. London: Williams & Norgate, Ltd., 1925.

_____. *What is Christianity?* London: Williams & Norgate, 1901.

Von Mosheim, John Laurence. *Institutes of Ecclesiastical History*. 4 vols. London: Longman, Brown, Green & Longmans, 1845.

Wace, Henry, and Schaff, Philip, eds. *A Select Library of the Nicene and Post-Nicene Fathers*. Vol. 1: *Eusebius' Church History*. Translated by Arthur Cushman McGiffert, 1890.

Warren, F.E. *The Liturgy and Ritual of the Ante-Nicene Church*. London: Society for Promoting Christian Knowledge, 1897.

Weiss, Johannes. *Earliest Christianity*. 2 vols. New York: Harper & Brothers, 1959.

Wellhausen, Julius. *History of Israel*. Edinburgh: Adam & Charles Black, 1885.

Wright, George Ernest, and Folson, Floyd Vivian, eds. *The Westminster Historical Atlas to the Bible*. London: S.C.M Press, Ltd., 1945.

Index

History, cutting oneself off from, 17
Holy Ghost: guidance of, is essential,
37; in early church, 37-38; Paul
was guided by, 38-39

Irenaeus, 14

James, 32, 58
Jesus Christ: beauty of teachings of,
2-3; visited spirits in prison, 13-16;
second coming of, Paul preached
of, 43, 48
Jews: gospel was preached first to, 27;
reluctance of, to abandon Mosaic
law, 28-29, 34; Christian, were
denied temple rights, 58
Journal, importance of keeping, 18

Keys, restoration of, 16-17
Kimball, Spencer W., 1

Law alone cannot save, 53-54, 60
Levitical priesthood, perfection came
not by, 59, 61
Light: children of, 3; filling whole
bodies with, 9
Light of Christ, 9
Love, gospel centers in, 54-55

Malachi, curse of, 17
Metaphor, Paul's use of, 62-63
Missionary work: quotation from
President Kimball on, 1;
throughout entire world, 19;
political barriers to, 21; among
diverse cultures, 56-57
Morality, Paul preached of, 47
Mosaic law, 59-61

Natural man: limits of, 7; refining of,
10
Neighbor, Paul's concept of, 54-55

Nephites, records of, 17-18
New Testament, 2

One body and one faith, 40
Opposition, role of, 5-6
Ordinances, performing of, for dead,
16
Origen, 16

Paganism, 34; Paul's teachings
against, 47-48
Palestine in Saul's day, 26-27
Paul: virtues of, 3; prophesied of
apostasy, 5, 42; Saul's name
changed to, 31; first missionary
journal of, 31-32; second
missionary journey of, 33; third
missionary journey of, 33-35;
epistles of, 35; persecution and
imprisonment of, 35; execution of,
36; received guidance from the
Holy Ghost, 38-39; was "all things
to all men," 41; recognized
universality of gospel, 52-53;
metaphors used by, 62-63. *See also*
Saul
Perfection: working toward, 45-46; of
saints, church is for developing,
48-49; came not by Levitical
priesthood, 59, 61
Persecution of saints, Paul's
prophecies concerning, 5
Peter, 29, 32, 38
Pharisees, 27
Philip, 28
Physical impulses, 8
Political barriers to missionary work,
21
Pride, corrupting power of, 9
Prophets, faith of, 50

Index

Records, importance of, 17-18

Refiner's fire, 10

Repentance: man's dependence on, 6; connection of, with atonement, 10-11; Paul's teachings concerning, 50

Resurrection, Paul's teachings concerning, 44-45

Revolution, technological, 17

Sadducees, 27

Salvation: for dead, 12-16, 18; gift of, 45; working out our own, 46; comes not by law, 53-54

Samaritans, preaching of gospel to, 28

Saul, 26; vision of, on road to Damascus, 30; name of, changed to Paul, 31. *See also* Paul

Sealing power, keys of, 13, 16-17

Smith, Joseph, 6

Smith, Joseph F., 15-16

Social and political customs,

separating, from gospel, 22-23

Sorrow, godly, 50

Spirit of God: man's dependence on, 6-7; searcheth all things, 8. *See also* Holy Ghost

Spiritual sensitivity, 8

Stephen, 28, 30

Technological revolution, 17

Temple, Jewish Christians were banished from, 58-59

Tertullian, 13

Thorn in the flesh, 10

Timothy, Paul's warnings to, 5, 42

Tribulation, glorying in, 5-6

Vision: of Peter involving unclean food, 29, 38; of Saul on road to Damascus, 30

Worship, essential aspects of, 23

Zion, 3, 62